Sowing the Seeds of Wonder

Discovering the Garden
in Early Childhood Education

www.lifelab.org

National Gardening Association's

www.KidsGardening.org
www.GardeningWithKids.org

Life Lab Science Program inspires learning and conservation by engaging students and educators in the natural world.

Life Lab has won awards and recognition from the National Science Teachers' Association, the National Science Foundation, the National Science Resources Center/Smithsonian Institute, the California School Board Association, the U.S. Department of Education, and the National Academy of Sciences.

Life Lab is a nonprofit organization located in Santa Cruz, California. Life Lab provides land-based educational programs for youth, and curriculum and professional development for educators. Life Lab created and operates the Life Lab Garden Classroom, a two-acre demonstration garden located at, and developed in collaboration with, the University of California Santa Cruz Center for Agroecology and Sustainable Food Systems (UCSC CASFS). In 2006, the Life Lab Garden Classroom was designated a Garden-Based Nutrition Regional Training Center by the California Department of Education.

PRINCIPAL CONTRIBUTORS
Erika Perloff
Amy Carlson
Jill Begin

CONTRIBUTORS AND SUPPORT
Deborah Bolt
Janine Canada
Whitney Cohen
Karen Doeblin

Jennifer Eckert
John Fisher
Juliana Grinvalsky
Gail Harlamoff
Janice Martinez
Barbara Kay Velez
Kim Woodland
Many lessons herein are
  adapted from Life Lab's
  Family Science Series

PROJECT TEAM
Editor: Whitney Cohen
Illustrations: Kate Murray;
  Erika Perloff; Life Lab logo
  and accompanying art, Sharon
  Erspamer; additional illustra-
  tions by the National
  Gardening Association
Design: Alison Watt, National
  Gardening Association

PHOTOGRAPHY: Life Lab or as noted.
p. 1 — St. Hilda's & St. Hugh's School
p. 21 (clockwise from left) — Life Lab, Hartnell College Child Development Center, Child's Play, Life Lab
p. 33 — John Fisher/Life Lab and Alicia Dickerson/Life Lab
p. 45 (clockwise from left) — Alicia Dickerson/Life Lab, Hartnell College Child Development Center,
  St. Hilda's & St. Hugh's School
p. 61 — Alicia Dickerson/Life Lab and Life Lab
p. 73 — (clockwise from top) Suzanne DeJohn/National Gardening Association; Life Lab and Alicia
  Dickerson/Life Lab
p. 87 — Alicia Dickerson/Life Lab

Published by the National Gardening Association, 1100 Dorset Street, South Burlington, Vermont 05401. (802) 863-5251. All rights reserved.

The National Gardening Association (NGA) is a nonprofit organization established in 1972. Its mission is to promote home, school, and community gardening as a means to renew and sustain the essential connection between people, plants, and the environment. NGA's programs and initiatives are targeted to five areas: plant-based education, health and wellness, environmental stewardship, community development, and responsible home gardening. For more information on the National Gardening Association and its programs, please visit *www.garden.org* and *www.kidsgardening.org*.

ISBN 978-0-915873-54-8
Library of Congress Control Number: 2009943688

Contents

APPENDIX

RESOURCES FOR PRESCHOOL GARDENING

GARDENING HOW-TO'S

BUILDING PLANS

ENGLISH/SPANISH VOCABULARY LIST

HARTNELL COLLEGE CHILD
DEVELOPMENT CENTER

Foreword

I well remember my first visit to Green Acres School in Santa Cruz, CA, where Life Lab began its first school garden in 1979. Even then, I was truly impressed by the scope of vision and hands-on dedication of the Life Lab staff. As the issues of childhood health and nutrition have grown over the years into the overwhelming challenges we face today, I fully appreciate the foresight of the Life Lab founders in recognizing the value of innovative, garden-based outdoor education.

Sowing the Seeds of Wonder is especially timely. To my knowledge, it is the first substantial early childhood gardening curriculum guide to be published, and it comes when the importance of literally sowing the seeds of healthy habits in the first years of life is beginning to be recognized.

Innate curiosity about nature is readily demonstrated in the first year of life. If you need proof, sit with a child in front of a midsummer perennial bed and watch what her hands and eyes do. Born curious, like nascent scientists, children explore nature because it has a unique capacity to stimulate their motivation to discover and acquire the particular tacit knowledge that flower and vegetable gardens offer. Rich, sensory gardening experiences early on help children grow up understanding that this is the way the world should be: colorful, fragrant, attractive to touch, tasty.

Furthermore, many educators have become convinced that if young children garden every day, learning that food comes from plants; that they can cook for themselves; that the results taste good; and that it is fun; then they are more likely to retain these healthy behaviors through childhood years and beyond. Playing and learning outdoors also motivates physical activity and fosters skills across all domains of child development.

Childcare or child development centers are differ-

HARTNELL COLLEGE CHILD DEVELOPMENT CENTER

ent from schools. Children are younger, emerging from Piaget's sensorimotor stage and entering the remarkable preoperational stage of development, where direct experience and sensory stimulation are imperative dimensions of healthy development. For preschoolers, learning is about moving, playing, and engaging with their immediate surroundings to discover what they have to offer. Gardens are unique in this regard as they provide a constantly changing diversity of vegetables and flowers that help children to become emotionally attached to nature.

Two thirds of the nation's children (9 million) attend some sort of early childhood program. If they start in their first year, full day, that's almost as many hours as the rest of their school career through high school. Furthermore, childcare is a highly regulated, state policy-sensitive sector of children's daily life. This means that system-wide adoption of site-level environmental and curricular innovation has the potential to generate enormous positive impact.

Research at the Natural Learning Initiative shows that many early childhood educators need help to overcome anxieties of working with children in nature. *Sowing the Seeds of Wonder* will help dispel commonplace myths and phobias that stop educators from getting their hands in the dirt, sowing seeds, harvesting, eating, and enjoying the fruits of natural labor.

Sowing the Seeds of Wonder challenges all of us involved in early childhood education to use the book as a tool to change day-to-day practice and system-level policy to incorporate a garden into every early childhood site to support healthy child development and a healthy planet.

Robin Moore
Director, The Natural Learning Initiative
Professor, North Carolina State University

The Art of Age-Appropriate "Gardening"

EARLY CHILDHOOD CENTER, UC SANTA CRUZ

ALICIA DICKERSON/LIFE LAB

"I'm doing an apple tasting during circle time with two year olds," says Jennifer Eckert of the Toddler Two's Center at UC Santa Cruz. She uses three apples: Big Yellow, Big Green, and Little Red and Yellow. Varieties are unimportant because what she's sharing with the children, subtly, are the colors. "During the tasting we also feel, smell, and listen to the crunch of the apples," she explains. "I ask the children what they *think* the apples will taste like, then *how* they taste. 'It tastes beautiful!' 'It tastes like apple juice!' they reply. I ask if the children have ever tasted strawberries, peaches, raspberries, or pears, and I say that these fruits are brothers and sisters of apples. I ask, *Do you eat apples at home? What do you think is inside the apple?* To this question, a chorus of children always sing out 'SEEDS!'"

After discovering apples with their senses, the children eagerly plant apple seeds in the soil and cover them up. Jennifer talks with them about what seeds need to grow: sun, water, soil, and air. The children carry cups of water from the spigot to where they planted the apple seeds. Some children water the seeds for 10 minutes — hours in toddler time! During this activity wonderful learning takes place: science, math, social interactions, cognitive and emotional growth, fine and gross motor development. (*Note:* Modern apple varieties are not grown from seed but rather are grafted. To grow an apple tree, choose a variety you like and plant an already grafted tree next to the apple seeds planted by the children.)

This activity is age appropriate. It takes place outside, so that children who can't sit still can come and go as they please. The children use all of their senses, which is primarily how young children learn about the world around them. Jennifer asks open-ended questions to see what they understand, and uses their answers to further their discussion and make their discoveries relevant to their lives.

Jennifer cautions that ECE teachers can't be too attached to the way their garden looks, or even to plants making it through the day. Plants and bugs get sacrificed. Young children learn to care for the garden by interacting with it, often with unintended consequences. The Toddler Two's simple curriculum of exploring, planting, and watering seeds occurs over several months, so the garden is usually overgrown. "Nonetheless," Jennifer says, "we have a bountiful supply of highly engaged and curious children."

When "gardening" with very young children, Jennifer recommends the following:

❋ Young children want to do everything themselves! Let them. Choose gardening activities that allow children to participate fully, to get messy, break leaves, step on plants, and feel that they have been completely successful.

❋ Young children have short attention spans and may not stick with an activity. It's helpful to follow age recommendations for activities.

❋ Sing, dance, use props, and tell stories!

❋ Plan activities in advance. You may lose children's attention if you leave them standing around while you retrieve something you need.

❋ Keep activities simple and share ideas in steps: here is a fruit, seeds are inside, plant seeds, water seeds, watch seeds grow, take care of the seeds. Each step takes time.

❋ Have fun! Exploration of the senses and of things wild and weedy are always exciting for children.

Introduction

In a preschool play yard nearby, Isabel is turning over the soil with a small hand trowel while Dylan carefully rescues worms and places them out of the way. Jessie sprinkles birdseed on a patch of bare dirt and packs it down well, wondering what will grow from these mysterious seeds. Monica and Joaquin are playing intently under some bushes, with tiny people they have fashioned out of sticks and flowers. Today their teacher will help them harvest the sunflowers they grew, and show them how to eat the seeds and make the heads into natural bird feeders. Their chatter reflects the learning that is taking place. "I am going to grow corn so high, it will be up into the sky!" "Look, the water all went away into the dirt." "This plant is all dead. How come it died?" Without a lot of instruction, these children are exploring and discovering the natural world through a small patch of garden. They are making connections between the food they eat for lunch and the seeds they plant. They are taking care of a small piece of the planet and making it more beautiful.

The simple act of cultivating a garden can open up a world of growth, learning, and enjoyment. It also provides children with a delicious introduction to healthy eating. Children who garden love to "graze" on tomatoes, green beans, and carrots. Children are much more likely to eat vegetables when they have grown them themselves, and take great pride in contributing to the family table or the classroom salad.

A garden for young people rarely resembles a typical adult garden. It might appear as small plots of earth with plants crowded in every which way. Plastic dinosaurs may creep through lettuce forests, nibbling as they go. Seeds often sprout up from the pathways where they've been spilled, and sometimes the plants that grow from them are the best in the garden. Leaves become blankets for dolls, and flowers become pots for miniature tea parties set among the bushes. The garden is a place for young children to play, to dream, to plant, to harvest and enjoy fresh produce, and to begin to know the workings of the natural world.[1]

The Life Lab Approach to Garden-Based Learning

Life Lab is a nonprofit organization based in Santa Cruz, California. We have been bringing learning to life in gardens since the first Life Lab school garden was established in 1979. True to our roots, we continue to run year-round field trips and summer camps for kids of all ages at our Garden Classroom in Santa Cruz. We also support schools and organizations across the country as they endeavor to begin or enhance their own garden-based learning programs.

Our work is inspired by the hope that all children — whether from urban centers or rural communities — will have the opportunity to develop an intimate connection to the natural world and, specifically, to their own local environment. A preschool garden allows young children to watch a place change throughout the seasons, and even throughout the years. As students engage with this place, they develop a profound empathy and love for it, and a sense of belonging somewhere. As they watch a spider weave her web or warm up a worm bin with a blanket of fallen leaves, children take the initial steps across the divide that

CHILD'S PLAY EARLY LEARNING CENTER, INC.

often separates people from place. As our students grow into decision-makers in their communities and beyond, their empathy and love for the natural world will serve as a foundation for a sense of responsibility and a determination to act on behalf of the environment.

Since the goal of an early childhood education garden is to create a space for joy, exploration, learning, and connection with living things, it is not necessary that you have a "green thumb" to get started. In fact, gophers, weeds, and other factors that might be devastating to a well-manicured botanical garden or a production farm can provide some of the most exciting learning opportunities in a children's garden. In the garden, your job is not to know the name of every plant and keep everything in perfect order. Rather, it is to serve as a guide to the children, to help them get started, and to keep them safe. Remember that the act of mucking around with soil, seeds, fresh air, and growing things is just as important as the final harvest. Along the way, seedlings may be eaten by birds, stepped on by little feet, or overwatered and washed away. If you can help turn these events into moments of discovery and learning, and can help the child get started again, you will teach a life-long lesson on how we learn and grow from our experiences. One Life Lab teacher's best garden experience began when she said, "That bird must have been really hungry to eat all our baby peas! What can we do next time to protect them?" and let the students work together to create a barrier to protect their new baby plants.

JOHN FISHER/LIFE LAB

Your students will have many questions once they begin their explorations. You do not need to have all the answers, just a willingness to discover along with them. Perhaps the best answer you can give to their gardening queries is "I don't know, let's find out together!"

Notes:

[1] For a summary of research regarding the impact of garden-based learning on childrens' academic achievement, nutrition, and social behaviors, visit: *www.csgn.org/research.php*

How to Use the Activities

This activity guide is designed to help you introduce young children to the joys of gardening. The simple activities provide a jumping-off place to explore the garden, whether it is a small schoolyard patch, a window box, or a well-established garden area. These activities can be done with very little gardening space and without expensive tools. We suggest recycled materials throughout, as children are just as happy gardening in old milk-cartons as in expensive pots.

Activities. All activities have a simple guide to help with planning as outlined in the example at right.

The code words above each activity title suggest:

* recommended **age levels**
* where the activity can be conducted: **inside** or **outside**
* the **season** best suited for the activity (this may vary by region)

The activities provide opportunities for integrating early concepts in science, math, language, movement, and art. Children learn new words, practice scientific process skills such as observation and classification, begin simple experiments, and create snacks and art in and from the garden.

Appendix. The appendix includes an extensive list of children's songs and literature that tie into the activities, so that, whenever possible, you can use picture books, music, and poems to extend the discoveries in the garden. You'll also find other resources for gardening with preschool-aged children, general gardening how-to information, and equipment designs.

RECOMMENDED AGES: 4+ ✽ INSIDE / OUTSIDE ✽ SEASON

Activity Title

DESCRIPTION	The activity and its purpose are briefly described.
BACKGROUND	If needed, background information is provided.
MATERIALS	All necessary materials are listed.
PREPARATION	All preparation steps are described.
ACTIVITY	The activity steps are listed.
TYING IT TOGETHER	Discussion questions or wrap-up activities are suggested. These are designed to allow students to reflect on what they have experienced, seen, and learned.
DIGGING DEEPER	Additional ideas related to the activity are suggested as follow-up lessons.

Getting Started

Outdoor garden classrooms come in all shapes and sizes. Life Lab has developed the following suggestions to help you get started, whether you hope to install a large garden, a rooftop greenhouse, or a planter box outside your front door.

Gathering a Team

Teamwork is an essential component of a thriving school garden program. Identifying supporters who are solidly behind your program should be your very first step. Consider asking the following people to join your garden team:

Administrators. An enthusiastic and supportive principal or director is key to the development of a school garden, from approving and arranging teacher time for workshops, to finding and tapping outside funding sources. Your director can also be an important school garden advocate outside of your school — an ambassador to your community and/or school district. It is essential that the principal or director be in full support of the garden, and ideally he or she will participate in the planning and implementation of a garden program.

Other school administrators can also play an important role, as can your local government officials and even state and federal legislators. It's worth your while to welcome superintendents, assistant directors, board members, or local policy makers into your school garden "family." Invite them to your groundbreaking or dedication ceremony. Send project updates regularly to keep their attention, and welcome them to observe firsthand how garden activities enhance classroom instruction and student learning.

Teachers. At most schools, a core group of teachers will be the catalyst for a school garden program. These teachers, often with the principal or school director and a few parents, will serve as the central organizing body that gets your garden growing. This planning or steering committee will work with other teachers, students, and staff members to determine what the school garden will look like, how it will be used, what resources and materials to collect, and who will accomplish which tasks.

Once the school garden plan is in place, the steering committee will oversee development and maintenance, evaluate successes, troubleshoot, and organize volunteers and community support. If your principal or director can't be a regular member of your planning team, be sure he or she is kept up to date on its progress. Some schools also include custodians on their steering committees, especially if their role will be important in implementation and maintenance. As you develop your plans, be sure they are incorporated into your school's short- and long-range goals and objectives.

Parents and volunteers. Many preschools or ECE childcare centers are small, with no more than two or three teachers. In all preschools, but especially small ones, the parents of your students will be crucial to launching and sustaining a garden project. Hold a parent-teacher meeting explaining the project and asking them to be on your steering committee. Involving parents from the very beginning will empower them to take action in their child's education and will give you some much-needed support.

Parents and other volunteers are a major part of successful school garden programs. Volunteers can help you build a tool shed or fence, organize a fundraiser to pay for a garden aide, contribute gardening expertise, or help you in the classroom. For many schools this volunteer support takes the form of an enthusiastic community support committee, often made up of parents. But don't worry if you don't have a huge committee to begin with; it should grow with your garden.

Keep parents informed as you plan your outdoor classroom. Send home flyers letting them know about your new outdoor classroom and how they might get involved. Ask them for specific types of expert help, such as in gardening, design, or carpentry, and donations of tools, materials, and supplies.

Some schools have found enthusiastic and knowledgeable volunteers in local garden clubs. Area educational institutions (universities, community colleges, and high schools) are also good sources, as are teacher education and science departments. Environmental studies and horticulture departments often offer internships, work study programs, or other community involvement opportunities to their students. Local senior citizens organizations are yet another source to tap.

Your county's Cooperative Extension Office is designed to provide various types of assistance to enterprises like yours. Some of the programs it coordinates,

including 4-H Clubs and master gardener programs, have provided assistance to school garden programs.

Regular volunteer meetings not only allow you to discuss activities and address problems and questions, but also let the volunteers know how valuable they are to your program. Make volunteer appreciation a major theme of garden events and have your students help write thank you letters to volunteers.

CERTIFICATE OF APPRECIATION THIS IS TO CERTIFY THAT Sam Mattern WAS A GREAT VOLUNTEER AND HELPED TO MAKE OUR GARDEN GROW. Signed: Kathy, Patti, Date: 5-7 Bobby, Jeffrey, Jane

CHECKLIST FOR GARDEN SITE DEVELOPMENT

ADVANCE WORK
* Form a planning committee of teachers, administrators, parents, and community members.
* Select the garden site. The site must get at least six hours of sunlight, have access to water, and be visible from classrooms.
* Design a garden plan. Designate:
  – garden areas, classroom beds
  – paths
  – tool shed/storage area
  – (optional) greenhouse/cold frame area
  – compost area
  – outdoor classroom area with tables and shade
  – water system
  – sink area and drinking fountain
  – needed fences (if any)
* Purchase tools and materials

BREAKING GROUND
* Organize a community work day
* Order seeds
* Acquire plants
* Rototill area if needed
* Stake garden beds to dig in ground, or build raised beds
* Do a preliminary soil test
* Add general soil amendments
* Establish a compost pile

ONGOING GARDENING
* Plant seeds in flats, six packs, or other containers
* Cultivate garden beds
* Plant and transplant

MAINTENANCE
* Water plants as needed
* Weed beds
* Provide protection from pests and harsh weather
* Harvest crops
* Maintain compost pile
* Plant cover crops
* Mulch beds

Establishing a Common Vision

It is helpful at the outset to work with your team to establish the purpose of your garden. Gather the people involved in the garden and ask yourselves: Why are we interested in gardening with our students? Why does our school have a garden, or, why is our school considering having a garden? How can we use a garden as an outdoor classroom? How will the garden integrate with the existing goals of our education center?

Making a Plan

Dream big, but start small. It is essential for your program that you start with a vision that excites all stakeholders, and is also manageable for all of the people involved. Consider developing a three-year plan for your garden, with realistic objectives for each year. While you may have visions of a mini-farm on the back parking lot or a greenhouse for those cold winter months, the best way to realize your dreams may be to start with a single garden bed and a compost bin. Remember, a tremendous amount of learning and discovery can happen with just a few seeds, a watering can, and small patch of earth.

Selecting the Site

Thriving school gardens come in all shapes and sizes, from a set of planter boxes on blacktop to an edible jungle overtaking the corner of a field. A dedicated team can transform almost any site, from a dirt parking lot to a school courtyard, into a flourishing outdoor classroom. Whether large or small, here are a few things to consider when choosing your garden site.

Sunlight. Most flowers and vegetables need a minimum of six hours of full sun per day. Check your future garden site for sun exposure at different times of the day and, if possible, in different seasons. Keep track of shady spots. Use them for observation areas, or gathering areas for hot, sunny days.

Water. Watering the garden is important for a good harvest, so select a site close to a water spigot, where watering will be hassle-free. There are various irrigation systems to consider: drip irrigation, overhead watering, or watering cans. Using a timer, you can deliver water to the garden on a regular basis without watering it by hand. It is always important, however, that someone check the garden regularly to ensure that the plants are receiving the water they need.

Soil. Plants need healthy soil to grow well. To ensure that your garden is as safe as possible, we recommend adhering to organic gardening practices, as described in Tips for Creating a Healthy Garden Ecosystem (p. 110). If you are starting a new garden in an area that may have toxic substances in the soil, such as an urban, industrial area, have the soil professionally tested for lead or other contaminants. If your soil is toxic, it's important to keep the entire garden in containers over paved ground, so the toxins cannot leach into the soil in the beds. Fill these container beds with a topsoil mix from a local landscape supply company. If your native soil is fine, then simply prepare it for planting, as described in Preparing In-Ground Garden Beds (p. 93).

Drainage. Both slope and soil type affect drainage. Avoid steep slopes; if that's not possible, consider terracing or building flat, raised beds. Don't plan a garden in a low spot where puddles form in wet weather.

Accessibility. Locating a garden close to the classroom makes it convenient, visible, and easy to incorporate into the curriculum on a regular basis. Student management will be easier, too. For preschool groups, garden beds or planter boxes right outside the classroom work especially well.

Security. If possible, locate your garden within sight of classrooms and neighbors. Fences and natural borders of plants, if they don't obstruct visibility and hide intruders, provide security. Make use of existing fences, trees, and hedges when selecting your site. Student-made signs at the garden's entry can help to deter vandals. An example might be: "Welcome to our garden! Please enjoy your stay, and leave it as you found it."

Visibility. Gardens always add beauty to school grounds. Try to integrate your garden with the existing landscape, but don't hide it. "Out of site, out of mind" can apply to gardens that aren't in a central, visible location.

Elements and Design

Once you've selected the site, it's time to design and map the garden itself. Think back to your own childhood and try to recall being in a garden or outdoor setting. What experiences do you remember most fondly? Most people who had early garden experiences recall places to hide, natural materials for building and play, elements that delighted the senses, and eating fresh food. Incorporating such elements into your garden helps to nurture children's love for building, playing, and learning with natural materials. Our sample garden plan (opposite page) may spark ideas.

Sample School Garden

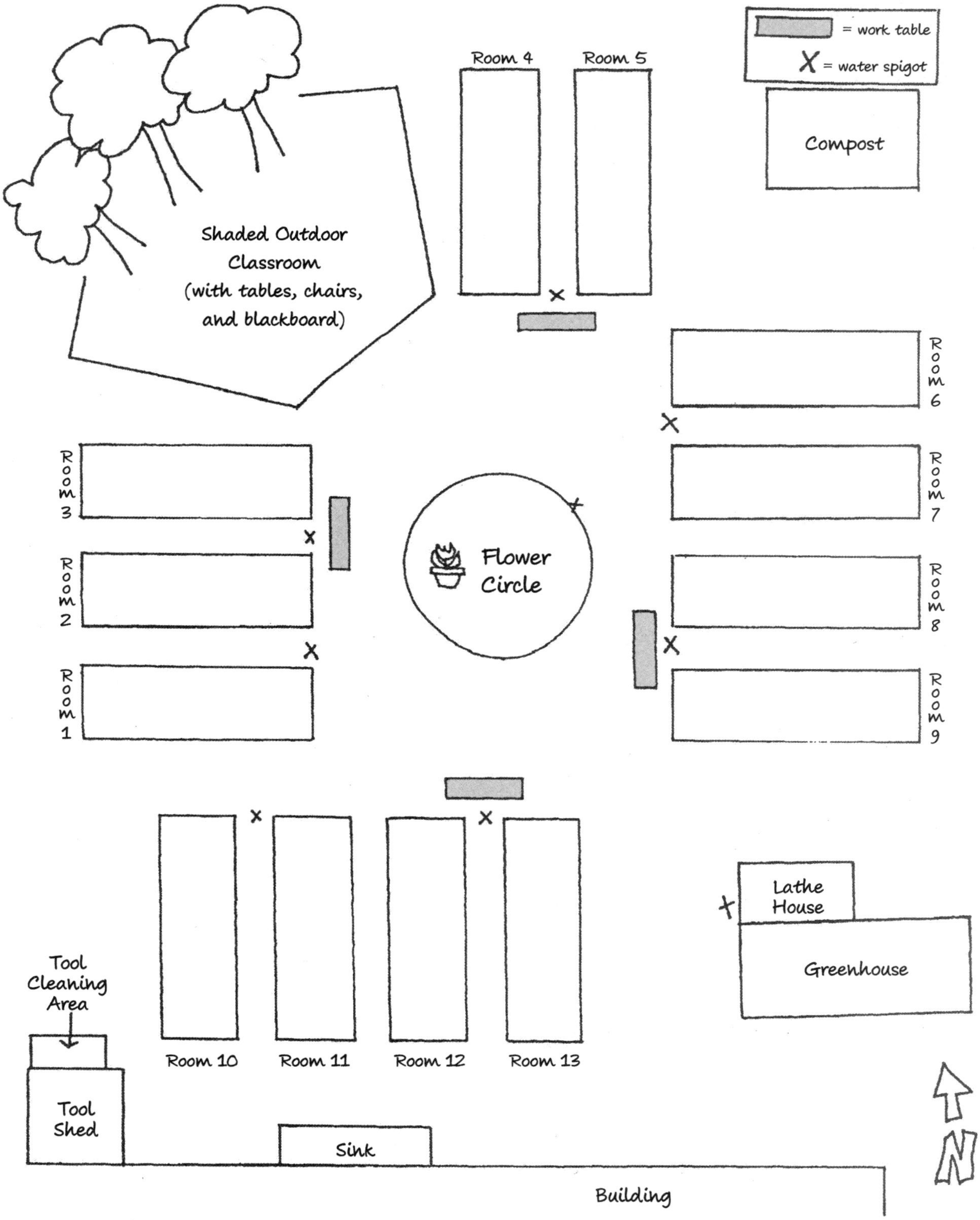

= work table

X = water spigot

Compost

Room 4

Room 5

Shaded Outdoor
Classroom
(with tables, chairs,
and blackboard)

X

Room 6

Room 3

X

Flower
Circle

X

Room 7

Room 2

Room 8

X

X

Room 1

Room 9

X

X

Lathe
House

X

Greenhouse

Tool
Cleaning
Area

Room 10

Room 11

Room 12

Room 13

Tool
Shed

Sink

Building

N

ALICIA DICKERSON/LIFE LAB

Outdoor classroom and meeting area.
Designate a shaded area with adequate seating for class discussions, writing, and drawing. An area with deciduous trees works well — in winter, you will have light and warmth; in summer you'll have shade. A dry-erase board attached to one side of the shade structure or tree is useful for instruction. Carpet squares, benches, or small stumps all make nice seating options.

Beds or planting areas. Make each bed two to three feet wide so that young children can work from either side without stepping on the plants or compacting the soil. These can be raised beds surrounded with a border of wood, cinder blocks, or recycled materials, or they can be beds dug directly in the ground. In either case, try to delineate the beds from the rest of the garden by using distinct material for the pathways or by lining the beds with string, flagging, or stones.

Theme beds. Theme beds are a great way to organize plants in a children's garden. You can grow all the ingredients needed for a recipe in a single bed, such as in a "Salsa Bed." Alternatively, you can plant an area of the garden to attract a certain animal, like a "Butterfly Bed." For more theme bed ideas, see Theme Bed Ideas (right).

Uncultivated digging pit. Young children love to play with soil. To honor this childhood delight and help garden plants survive, it's a good idea to create a designated space just for digging and playing. Leave an area of ground or a raised bed uncultivated and let the children explore in the dirt! This is a good option for a shaded part of the garden, since you're probably not trying to grow plants there.

Compost area. Walt Whitman said it all: "Behold this compost, behold it well, it grows such sweet things from such corruption." Composting is a fundamental garden activity and a way to recycle garden waste; and

on top of all that, it produces valuable soil amendments. Set aside an area for collecting compost materials and building compost piles. You can never have too much of this important garden ingredient. And, of course, don't forget the worms! Vermicomposting, or the use of worms for composting, is a wonderful element in any school garden. Consider using one or both of these approaches to compost. For more information on composting, see pages 106-109.

Tool shed or storage area. A tool shed or storage area provides a central location where you can clean, organize, and protect tools and equipment. If you're purchasing a new shed, consider one with a skylight so you can see inside without electricity.

Sink. For convenience, plan to incorporate a sink into your garden. A multi-faucet sink is great for washing little hands or filling watering cans. Until you can install the sink, keep a 5-gallon water cooler (with lid) on a table in your garden. When you are working with kids in the garden, fill the cooler with a garden hose and use the spigot at the bottom as a water faucet where kids can wash their hands or fill small watering cans. Because of safety regulations involving young children and pools of water, always keep the lid on the cooler, watch the cooler closely when it's full, and empty it after every use.

Optional Design Extras

Once your basic garden is established, any of these design extras can be a very special addition.

Greenhouse or coldframe. A greenhouse or

Theme Bed Ideas

Sample Edible Theme Beds
Salsa bed: Tomatoes, tomatillos, onions, garlic, cilantro
Salad bed: Lettuce, radishes, carrots, beets, nasturtiums, celery, spinach
Three sisters bed: Popcorn, pole beans (these can grow up the corn stalks), winter squash

Sample Literature Theme Bed
Tops and Bottoms (by Janet Stevens): Carrots, radishes, beets, lettuce, broccoli, celery

Sample Art and Whimsy Bed
Edible rainbow flower bed: Red nasturtiums, orange and yellow calendula, green basil, blue bachelor buttons, purple chive flowers

6-foot bamboo poles or broomsticks

Pole Beans

coldframe is a protected place for starting seedlings in a controlled environment. Coldframes also help to extend the growing season during the cooler months. Alternatively, you can set up an indoor growing area in your classroom for the same purpose. See Building a Coldframe for Your Garden (p. 112).

Tepee. Growing vines up the poles of a tepee creates a special place for children to hide in. With its circular shape, a tepee also doubles as a fun meeting spot. Any kind of bean that can be eaten raw makes a classic tepee vine; however, any climbing vine can work well on a tepee, so be creative!

Tunnel. Build a basic tunnel frame and grow a perennial vine over it to create a very special play space for children where their imaginations can run free. At Life Lab, our tunnels are covered in trumpet vine, thumbergia, and passionflower, and they come alive with pollinators in the spring and summer. Research which perennial climbing vines will grow best in your area. Many gardens call this design element a "Magic Tunnel."

Gourd dome. A gourd dome is a wonderful way of incorporating a playground-like element into your garden. Gather recycled bicycle rims and fasten them together with twine, or better yet, with recycled bicycle tubes. Use the rims to build a large dome, shaped like a small jungle gym (see photo, right) and plant gourds around the bottom edge. During the winter and spring, the dome acts like a jungle gym for children to play in and around. During the summer, gourd vines begin to cover the dome. The fall brings the most fun — ripening gourds hang down into the center of the dome like giant raindrops!

Tree-o-tunes. A tree-o-tunes is a fun and creative way to recycle in your garden. Choose a large tree in the garden distanced from the classroom and learning areas, or use any sort of structure if you have no trees. Then adorn the tree or structure with recycled instruments! Anything can make music — here are some ideas to get you started: snake a large plastic hose through the tree for amplified singing; attach a variety of pots and pans

to the tree like a set of drums; hang dry gourds for maracas; position an empty water drum upside-down and hit it with padded wooden dowels like a gong.

Raptor perches/owl boxes. Raptor perches and owl boxes can bring more birds to your garden, enrich your garden ecosystem, and control pests. Bird posts are a wonderful resting place for any bird and specifically — if the post is large enough — birds of prey. Position posts near open areas where birds of prey can catch mice and gophers. Place owl boxes in a quiet part of the garden, since owls sleep during the day. Your location will determine the types of owls you might attract, and thus the best dimensions for your box. You can purchase owl boxes or plans for your region at *www.hungryowl.org/boxes.html*. Once the box is installed, search for owl pellets under it and use sticks to explore the bones and fur in them with your students!

Bird feeders/houses. Bird feeders and birdhouses both attract beautiful winged visitors to the garden. It is important to place these in a different part of the garden than your raptor perches and owl boxes to ensure the safety of smaller winged visitors. For instructions on making bird feeders, see page 69.

Root view box. A root view box is a planting container with one clear side, where students can watch roots grow over time. For building plans, see page 115.

Chickens. Chickens add so much to an instructional garden! They provide eggs for eating, manure for the compost pile, and endless hours of joy and fascination for young children. To learn more about keeping chickens, visit *www.backyardchickens.com*.

Art and whimsy. An old school desk overflowing with growing flowers, a tile mosaic illustrating the process of pollination, colorful flags, murals, and other pieces of art and whimsy all inspire creativity in the garden. Include art made by local community members, as well as by your students.

Garden Signs

No matter what size your garden is, make a sign to give it an identity. Let your neighbors know what this new patch of greenery is all about. Signs help identify your garden as an outdoor learning center, announce times the garden is open, and provide rules and guidelines for using the space. The signs can be simple or complex — they just need to be clear. Signs are best when they represent the character of the class. Ask students to help decide what will appear on their sign. Sign making can be a great class project.

Raising Funds and More

Donations of money and materials from community members, businesses, and charitable organizations can enhance your outdoor classroom program tremendously. Fundraising may provide a garden aide's salary, tools and seeds, or reference books. Even if you can't get district funds for your outdoor classroom, there's a good chance you can get someone to donate many of the materials and much of the labor you need.

Because most teachers don't have time for a lot of fundraising, many schools rely on the assistance of parents and community support committees to guide fundraising efforts. Here are some strategies that Life Lab schools have found fruitful.

Start locally. While you may have heard about "all those big grants" available from the state and federal government, your best bet for school garden support is often right in your own backyard. Draw on any district funds that may be available. Ask your school's network for assistance. Start with parents and neighborhood businesses that have helped your school before.

The type of help easiest to get is a donation of goods or services, also known as "in-kind" contributions. Consider such sources as:

❀ Local businesses — nurseries, lumber companies, irrigation or bulldozing contractors; any business that has or does something you need. Bookstores are a possibility as you augment your garden-related book collection.

❀ Local farmers — parents or other school supporters in the farming business can be a valuable

ALICIA DICKERSON/LIFE LAB

source for services (rototilling), goods (seedlings, used tools, or even historic farm equipment for a display), and expertise.

❀ Garden clubs — members of these organizations can be sources of both expertise and gardening goods and services.

❀ Individuals — parents and other community members may present unexpected talents and resources. For example, at Palmetto School in Miami, Florida, local TV newscasters volunteered to work with students on a special project to study the weather.

Sometimes what you need is something a donor wants to give away. Be creative. One teacher reports that she makes the rounds of area pumpkin lots after Halloween and collects used bales of straw for mulch. Frank Porter Graham Elementary in Chapel Hill, North Carolina, has organized a post-Halloween "pumpkin drop" to collect compost material. Tree removal companies often donate wood chips for garden pathways.

Larger projects, such as building a greenhouse or putting in an irrigation system, may call for a more formal approach. In this case, develop a specific project proposal that includes a concise description of your project, a list of needed materials, and an estimated budget. Compile a list of businesses that could supply those materials and make appointments to meet with the owners or managers of those businesses.

In the meeting, describe the purpose of your garden as it relates to student learning. If possible, bring along photos of the site and samples of student work. Show your materials list and ask if the business can contribute any of the items on it. Don't get discouraged if early attempts are unsuccessful — fundraising can take time and perseverance.

For cash contributions, look to community service groups such as the Lions or Kiwanis clubs, waste disposal companies, PTA or PTO school improvement funds, or community foundation grants. Your local United Way will have information about community foundations in your area and about other sources of funding. Research whether or not your city sponsors beautification projects. For example, the San Francisco Green Schoolyard Alliance is a coalition of Bay Area civic organizations, schools, and government agencies that transform urban schoolyards from ordinary asphalt yards into ecologically rich green spaces.

TOD HADDOW/LIFE LAB

plans to discard plants, flats, or seedlings; landscape suppliers will often provide plants and gardening expertise; stables and farms can be a regular source of straw or compost. One Washington, D.C., school found that the local zoo was a valuable resource, providing masses of manure for the school compost pile.

Purchasing Tools and Materials

As you make a detailed list of the tools and materials you will need (see Basic Gardening Equipment, below), brainstorm ways to get them. Here are some things that might be on your list and ways that schools have acquired them.

Planter boxes and a tool shed. Approach a local lumber company about providing materials or offering a discount; a parent may have the skills to design the boxes or shed and/or lead a volunteer work party in constructing them.

Fencing. See if district funds are available, or seek donations of materials. Remember to include openings large enough for truck access. If possible, put your garden in a location that is already fenced, at least on one side.

Tools. Send a list home to parents, many of whom may have old tools to donate. Bring your list to a local garden supply business or a charitable organization, which might donate the tools. Many schools have found garden tools at local flea markets and garage sales; one school placed a small notice in the local newspaper and was given the contents of a barn full of equipment.

Be sure to buy quality tools, even though they cost a little more. Well-made tools will hold up under the wear and tear youngsters often give them. Look for plastic, dull-edged hand trowels, and other tools made for young children at *www.gardeningwithkids.org*.

You may find that you need to solicit large donations, such as if you plan to hire a garden coordinator. Here are some tips for applying for large grants:

❊ Find grants with requirements that match your needs.

❊ Do your homework. Research the programs supported in the past and the current priorities of the organization.

❊ Submit a professional application, making sure to follow all instructions, answer questions thoroughly, keep text concise and meaningful, and include plans for long-term sustainability.

❊ Ask someone to proofread you application before submitting it.

❊ Make sure the application is easy to understand. If you handed it to a stranger, would he or she be able to translate your goals and purpose?

❊ Submit the application before the deadline.

Keep a record of all donations. After you receive your funds or supplies, it's important to respond to every donation, regardless of size, with a thank you letter. Letters handwritten and illustrated by students are always nice. Many schools acknowledge large donations with a more elaborate thank you (including perhaps a certificate or plaque) incorporated into a special event at the school garden. In Santa Cruz, California, students at Branciforte Elementary School made tiles to thank their donors. The children used the tiles to make a decorative border on the outside of their tool shed.

With garden-related businesses, in particular, try to establish ongoing relationships. For example, encourage a local nursery to give you a call when it

Basic Gardening Equipment

shovels	tool cleaning brush
spades	hoses/nozzles
hoes	watering cans
spading forks	stakes
leaf rakes	twine/string
soil rakes	pruning shears/scissors
many hand trowels (plastic	rain gauge
is great for preschoolers)	compost thermometer
wheelbarrows	harvest baskets

Preparing the Garden Site

With your garden site plan in hand and tools rounded up, it's time to create your outdoor classroom.

Soil conditions. Establishing a garden begins with preparing the soil. Consider having your soil professionally tested for lead or other toxins. If the test is positive, it will be important to keep the entire garden in containers over paved ground, where the toxins cannot leach into the bed soil. Fill these containers with a topsoil mix from a local landscape supply company or make your own, using 5 parts compost, 4 parts garden soil, and 1 part sand.

For small in-ground sites with relatively loose soil you can turn the earth with spading forks and shovels. These tools get more people involved and are less expensive than using machines. If your site hasn't been gardened recently, the earth may be compacted. In this case you may opt to prepare the soil with a rototiller or small tractor and plowing attachment. In Pescadero, California, a local farmer spent an afternoon rototilling an old patch of lawn at a nearby school. When he left, the school had 12 new beds ready for amending and planting!

Staking out beds. Once your soil is loosened, mark off the garden plots with stakes and string. With plenty of volunteers on hand, locate and drive a stake into the corners of the overall garden area. Stretch twine from stake to stake, forming one large rectangle. Next, plot out the paths and beds. These can be rectangular, round, squiggly, spiral, or any other shape you want, but should be no more than two to three feet wide.

Bed Preparation. This is the most important step in the process of nurturing healthy soil. Good soil produces healthy, nutritious plants that are less prone to pest and disease problems. Some gardeners prefer to build beds with raised edges. Others prefer to garden in beds at ground level. If you choose raised beds, keep the edges low enough for students to easily reach into. You can build raised beds or purchase a wide variety of raised bed kits from garden supply centers or catalogs such as *www.gardeningwithkids.org*.

Whether you create raised or in-ground beds, you will want to prepare your soil before you plant. For information on soil and bed preparation, see Preparing In-Ground Garden Beds (p. 93).

What about the Summer and Holidays?

If you are able to maintain your garden lightly throughout the summer and during holidays, students will return to a bountiful fall harvest of crops, as well as plenty of weeds for the compost pile. However, garden maintenance, especially during summer and holidays, can be a challenge. Many of the schools we work with have devised creative solutions. Some schools invite city recreation programs to use the garden for an environmental education summer camp. At other schools, students and families water and maintain the garden for a week at a time in exchange for harvesting the wonderful summer crops and sharing in the adventure of gardening. Still other schools have timed irrigation throughout the summer, and come back in the fall to a very weedy, but abundant garden.

Student Management

Although the logistics of an outdoor classroom can be tricky, the rewards can be great. As Dr. Roger Johnson, Professor of Curriculum and Instruction and Co-director of the Cooperative Learning Center at the University of Minnesota puts it, "Once you see the excitement of a young child harvesting a first carrot, you have to wonder how education ever moved so far from its roots."

Safety in the Garden

When gardening with very young children, safety should be your foremost concern. Children need to learn proper behavior to keep themselves and others safe. The garden is a good place to teach these important lessons. Early on, teach children not to eat garden plant parts without adult permission — some weeds and plant parts (e.g., leaves, stems, roots) of even common garden vegetables, like tomatoes, can be toxic. Take special care not to use toxic plants in areas where infants and toddlers play (see Toxic Garden Plants & Fungi, p. 92).

Other safety precautions include gardening with kid-friendly tools (keep any adult tools out of children's reach). Provide dull-edged hand trowels for the children to work with. Always demonstrate how to use them safely, and especially how to dig into the soil without flinging dirt into anyone's faces. Older children can use larger tools with appropriate training on safe tool use and care.

In a children's garden, we recommend gardening without chemical pesticides and fertilizers. These products generally include warnings to keep them out of children's reach. For more information on how to create a thriving garden without using chemical pesticides and fertilizers, see Tips for Creating a Healthy Garden Ecosystem (p. 110).

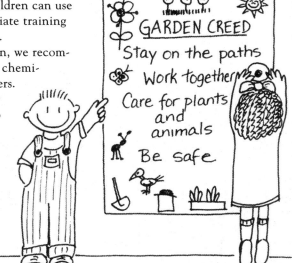

Remember that even natural pesticides can be toxic if ingested or handled. Be aware of water safety, as well. If adults aren't present, do not leave even small amounts of water in buckets or pools where small children play. Safe gardening also includes sun protection. Make sure children always apply sunscreen and provide sun hats while outside.

A Student-Centered Environment

It takes time for children to develop the ability to work cooperatively in an outdoor classroom setting. Once they get the hang of it, though, students develop greater independence and more cooperative skills each year for their ongoing explorations. Here are some tips:

Cooperative structures. Teachers who use Life Lab curriculum rely on a variety of small-group approaches to learning, many of which involve the techniques of cooperative learning. Breaking up the class into groups of three to five students can be very effective in an outdoor classroom setting. If you set up classroom stations for students to explore, each group can rotate through them. For young children this works best when each group has supervision.

Buddy classes. A "buddy class" system teams a lower-grade class with an upper grade one, matching students one-on-one for projects. If your preschool is located near an elementary, middle, or high school, this is a great option. The older students can lead their preschool "buddies" in a simple activity taught to them ahead of time. Many of the activities in this book are ideal for buddy classes.

Additional adults. Another way teachers manage class time in school gardens is by increasing the adult-to-student ratio. Some schools have a paid garden aide, while others make use of community volunteers and parents. If your volunteers will be helping with group management, have them observe the class until they feel comfortable supervising

HARTNELL COLLEGE CHILD DEVELOPMENT CENTER

a small group on their own. Keep the number of students per volunteer as low as possible.

Rules. Establishing and following rules helps with safety management. The garden is a special kind of classroom and requires special rules both for effective learning and safety. Set up a standard garden orientation program for students and another one for volunteers. Over the years, Life Lab has generated these basic rules:

* ✻ Always walk in the garden.
* ✻ Stay on the paths.
* ✻ Always ask an adult before using any tool or picking any plants.
* ✻ Always ask an adult before tasting anything.
* ✻ Respect plants, animals, and each other.

In addition, it's wise to create specific rules for using garden tools, and demonstrate to students proper and improper use of tools. Some teachers find it helpful to model correct and incorrect behavior and have students critique them. Your garden may require certain other rules, too, such as "Always keep the gate shut" or "Always wipe your feet and wash your hands before returning to class." Phrase the rules positively and try to keep them simple — the fewer the better. Inviting students to help develop these rules promotes greater understanding and follow-through. You can use the activity "Critter Crawl" (p. 63) to develop rules about respecting animals. Once you've discussed and demonstrated the rules, have students practice them together.

Post a list of your garden rules prominently, (e.g., on the door of your tool shed) and remind your students of them whenever they're in the garden. Consider illustrating each rule with a picture or drawing. Whether or not the children can read these rules, it's important to have them as a reminder to older students and adult volunteers.

Enjoying Food with Students

Enjoying a fresh harvest is one of the best parts of gardening with young children. Here at Life Lab, we taste all sorts of garden-fresh treats with students, and are often surprised to discover what they like! When eating with students it's important to honor preferences. We let students know up front that we hope they will try new things, but they will never have to finish anything they don't like. In fact, we tell children that if they taste anything they'd rather not finish, they can spit it right onto the ground, where it will go into the soil and help new plants grow. We have found that children, when given this freedom, feel less apprehensive about trying new fruits and vegetables. It is not uncommon for a child to leave a field trip here asking his or her parents to please buy some beets, winter squash, persimmons, or figs to have at home!

Getting to Know the Garden

Child's Play Learning Center

PICKERINGTON, OH

The Child's Play Learning Center serves children 6 weeks to 12 years old, and children older than 12 often stay with the program to help with the younger children. Owner and teacher Barbara Kay Velez Barbosa explains that although they've been gardening for a long time on their three-acre site, their garden remains a work in progress. "We began with a few flower beds around the school. We've added a butterfly garden with a bike path around it; a strawberry patch in an old wading pool; an herb garden in an old sensory table; a sunflower house made from string and bamboo; and a vegetable garden filled with cucumbers, zucchini, squash, corn, and green beans. The infants and toddlers garden in an old sand box. We plan to add more Ohio native plants and a rain garden to catch and use the runoff water from our picnic shelter. The more we garden, the bigger our garden gets!"

CHILD'S PLAY EARLY LEARNING CENTER, INC.

The school curriculum follows Ohio's educational standards and can be met in the garden, where the learning is experiential and hands-on. Children learn about how things grow, but they also learn that their hard work has positive, measurable results — an important life lesson. It takes a full school year to plan, plant, and harvest a garden, so it is a perfect setting for children to learn what they can accomplish over a period of time. "As our gardens have expanded," says Barbara, "we've watched the children grow developmentally and physically, and witnessed their academic achievements.

The children have many favorite garden activities. They divide perennials in spring, watch the divisions grow into full-sized, beautiful plants, then divide them again the next year to keep the cycle going. The children also start seeds indoors, check daily to see if they've peeked up through the dirt, then transplant the seedlings into the gardens. They water every day (sometimes too much) and weed the beds — although everyone accepts that the weeds will always grow back. The children love to explore the wildflower maze and discover new things in it. They harvest vegetables, do cooking activities at school, and take some vegetables home to their families. "This year," notes Barbara, "we also gave some of our produce to a homeless shelter. Each season brings new opportunities in the garden."

When gardening with children, Barbara says there are two critical things to bear in mind: always make it *fun* and don't expect perfection. Even with string as a guide, the rows of corn, peas, and beans will not be straight; the sunflowers will need a lot of thinning; and the pumpkins, gourds, squash, and zucchini will grow into the lawn, where they will sometimes be stepped on by small running feet.

"We've witnessed some wonderful moments in our gardens, but one I will cherish for years involved our pumpkin patch," shares Barbara. "After planting the pumpkins, we explained to the children that no fruits would develop if the vines or blossoms got trampled. One boy checked the pumpkins each morning to make sure the flowers and vines were intact. One day he came running, concerned that the flowers had died. But looking more closely, we showed him a baby pumpkin forming on the vine. After that, he checked the fruit's growth each morning. Finally it was ready to harvest, but he didn't want anyone to pick the pumpkin. He reasoned that because it had taken such a long time to grow, it deserved to rest for a while."

RECOMMENDED AGES: 4+ ❀ OUTSIDE ❀ ANY SEASON

Rainbow Chips

DESCRIPTION

In this activity, children use paint chips to search the garden for corresponding colors. This is a great way to introduce children to the garden and prompt a close look at the diversity of color.

BACKGROUND

The garden is teeming with color! Often we think of finding color only in flowers, but if we look closely at each plant, rock, and handful of soil, we can find every color of the rainbow. This activity is an excellent way to introduce young children to a garden and you can repeat it throughout the year as the seasons change. You can even talk about shades and tones of color. For example, there isn't just one green, there are many shades and tones of green. Pushing children's awareness of color in the garden helps them discover things they might otherwise overlook.

MATERIALS

❀ Variety of paint chip samples from a local paint or hardware store, cut up into individual color squares
❀ A bag or container in which to conceal the paint chips
❀ Tempera paints

ACTIVITY

Start by telling this imaginary story (embellished as you like!) in a mysterious tone of voice:

"One day I was walking through the garden, when it started to rain really hard. Soon enough, I was in the middle of a huge storm. With each step I took, I became more and more soaked. I continued to walk through the dark and wet garden, until I came to an open meadow. Above the meadow the sun started to peek out through the heavy clouds, and the rain settled down to a mist. Then, a huge double rainbow appeared over the hills in the distance. The colors were so vivid and bright. There were shades of red, orange, yellow, green, lime, peach, pink, purple, maroon, blue, turquoise, and cobalt. There were even colors in that rainbow that I hadn't seen before…colors without names. All of a sudden, the rainbow just shattered in the sky, and all the pieces fell to earth. I ran over to the pieces and began picking them up and putting them all in a bag. Would you all like to see the rainbow chips?"

Now have the students find a partner. If possible, assign an adult chaperone or older child to each group. Give each group a "rainbow chip" from your pouch and instruct the children to look for the exact color somewhere in the garden. Encourage them to look very closely at grains of soil, stripes in a tree's bark, and other places they might otherwise overlook and to try to find matches in the natural parts of the garden, rather than on signs or buildings. Show children how to hold the paint chip just behind the object to determine if they have a good match. Demonstrate how something red that they find could be a very different red from the color on the chip. *Does this match? How about this?* Then send students out with one color chip to look for their own good match. You may choose to have them show other students, or adults, their match in the place where they found it. Alternatively, you may ask students to bring their items back to the circle to share with the group. Either way, once they have found a good match, students can return the chip to your bag and select a new one. Repeat the activity four or five times per team.

TYING IT TOGETHER

Each time you do this activity, record the date and post all the colors the children found. Then ask, *What colors did you see most often in the garden? Is this different from the last time*
we did this activity? The children may see more green in the spring and summer, but possibly reds, yellows, and browns in the fall and winter.

Is there a place in your garden where the children might find concentrations of bright colors? How about dark colors? See if they can point out those spots.

Ask, *Is there a place in the garden where you think there isn't any color at all?* Go with the children to this place and help them find colors!

DIGGING DEEPER

Set up the paints and paper. Put out one basic paint color — red, orange, yellow, green, blue, purple, brown — and one tint — black or white. Let the children finger paint with those two paints on a piece of paper to explore the spectrum of that basic color. When the paintings are dry, you can repeat the activity with these homemade paint chips!

RECOMMENDED AGES: 4+ ✤ OUTSIDE ✤ ANY SEASON

Human Cameras

(Adapted from Joseph Cornell's *Sharing Nature with Children*, Volume 2)

DESCRIPTION   In this activity, children explore the garden while taking turns pretending to be a photographer or a camera. This activity encourages children to learn to use their sense of sight as they study the details of their garden.

BACKGROUND   The world is full of information for children to discover using all their senses. The eyes are often the first way we learn about a place and the objects in it. By pretending to be cameras and photographers, children and adults can look at the garden in a new way.

MATERIALS   ✤ (*Optional*) A working camera
✤ (*Optional*) Paper and painting supplies

PREPARATION   Find an area of the garden where children can walk easily without tripping. If possible, pair up each student with an adult helper or, better yet, with an older child. This activity works well during the school day, and can also be a great activity to send home with parents.

ACTIVITY   Invite the children to sit in a circle. Show them the camera and have a discussion about what a photographer is (someone who uses a camera to take a picture) and what a camera is (a tool for taking pictures). Ask the children, *Why would a photographer want to take pictures? Why are pictures important?* This conversation can be lively depending on the children's experiences.

Tell the children that today they will take turns pretending to be photographers and cameras in the garden. With their partner, they will visit the garden. The "photographer"

will find something to take a picture of and the "camera" will take the picture.

Show your students a camera shutter. Ask, *How are your eyes like a camera shutter?* (When a camera's shutter is open, a picture is collected. When your eyes are open, the pictures you see are sent to your brain and kept there.) Have the children open and close their eyes and imagine they are camera shutters. Ask, *How important are your eyes to you?* Tell the children, *This game gives you a chance to think about your eyes and how they connect you to the world.*

Ask the children to pick who will be the photographer and who will be the camera. Explain that the camera will keep his or her eyes shut while the photographer points it at something in the garden that he or she thinks will make a good photo and then pulls gently on the camera's earlobe to take the picture. Using a volunteer, demonstrate how to lead a partner with his or her eyes closed. Hold the hand and elbow of one arm and guide your camera very slowly. Make a point of giving the camera clear directions, checking the ground in front of the camera's feet, and going around obstacles. When the camera feels a gentle tug on his or her earlobe, that person opens his or her shutter (eyes) for a moment, and then closes them again. After taking three pictures this way, have the camera and photographer switch roles.

One picture might be a close-up. Explain that a close-up photograph shows details, like dew on the petals of a flower, or the way the stem is attached to a vegetable. Encourage the photographer to spend a few minutes looking for an interesting garden detail. Then have him or her focus the camera on the detail and take the picture.

Another picture might be taken from an unusual angle. Suggest that the photographer look at the garden from a different perspective. For example, the photographer could lie on the ground and look up. Have the photographer try looking at berries and leaves from this angle, or flowers. If there is a tree in the garden, try looking up at the sky through the leaves. Once the photographer has chosen the picture, have him or her set up the camera and take the picture.

Other photographic possibilities might include: bright colors in the garden, interesting arrangements of shapes or objects, insects in the garden, or people in the garden.

After each photograph is taken, have each child and his or her partner hold a short discussion to stay focused and to help the child remember the photograph. If the child was the camera, have the photographer walk the child away from the picture, then challenge him or her to find where the picture was taken. Then have the photographer compare what he or she saw to what the camera saw. *How are the two "pictures" different?*

TYING IT TOGETHER

When each person has had a chance to be both photographer and camera, discuss what it was like to take the pictures. Ask the children, *What did you notice about your garden that you hadn't noticed before? What was it like to be the camera? The photographer? What was your favorite picture?*

DIGGING DEEPER

Invite the children to show each other where their favorite picture was taken in the garden.

Set up a painting station and have the children make a painting of their favorite "photo."

With close adult supervision, let each child take one special photo in the garden with a real camera. Print the photos and use them to make a class book or poster about the garden.

RECOMMENDED AGES: 2¹/₂⁺ ❄ OUTSIDE ❄ ANY SEASON

Garden Creatures

DESCRIPTION

Children get to know the garden space by making tiny creatures out of odds and ends and finding homes for them in the garden. These "Garden Creatures" draw children's attention and imaginations to details of the garden that might otherwise be overlooked.

BACKGROUND

Gardens provide endless opportunities for children to discover and explore nature while developing an awareness of how it works. By placing a tiny "creature" in the garden world, they start to notice details such as the scale of plants, the texture of leaves, or the smells of flowers.

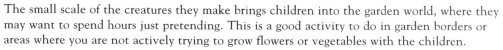

The small scale of the creatures they make brings children into the garden world, where they may want to spend hours just pretending. This is a good activity to do in garden borders or areas where you are not actively trying to grow flowers or vegetables with the children.

MATERIALS

❄ Newspaper
❄ A variety of small objects from the garden, such as walnut shells, dry sticks and leaves, stones, fruits, etc.
❄ Art supplies to decorate the objects, such as paint and paintbrushes, glue and googly eyes, pipe cleaners, etc.
❄ *The Snail's Spell* by Joanne Ryder

PREPARATION

Cover a table in newspaper and put out the small garden objects and the art supplies; pour glue into containers.

ACTIVITY

Gather the class around you and read *The Snail's Spell* to get the children thinking about being really small.

Tell the children they will be using everyday objects to make small "garden creatures," which will go with the children when they explore the garden. Show them the materials and help them think of ways to make the objects look like creatures by gluing on eyes, making arms from sticks, dresses from leaves, etc. Provide assistance as needed. Have the children think of names for their garden creatures and share them with the group.

Next tell the children it's time to find homes for their creatures in the garden. Establish safety rules for where the children can and can't go in the garden and help them find places to set up their creatures. Encourage the children to pick up and use fallen leaves and other natural materials for these "homes." They may want to make rooms under bushes or leaf beds, find "food," dig small pits for the creatures to play in, and more. Allow as much time as the children need to create the garden homes. The children's imagination and your tolerance for garden rearranging are the only limits. Observe the children to see how they interact with the plants, soil, and garden spaces. When you're done with the activity, collect all the creatures and bring them inside. It's fun to repeat the activity as the garden and seasons change.

TYING IT TOGETHER

When the children are together again, ask them to share some of the things they noticed in their garden areas. *How did one area differ from another? Do they want to visit their miniature garden homes again?* Invite the children to show each other their garden homes.

DIGGING DEEPER

Take time regularly for children to continue exploring the garden with their creatures. What do they notice as the seasons change? Based on the children's observations, encourage them to "renovate" their homes to adapt to the seasons (make rain shelters, warmer beds, etc.).

Encourage the children to work together to create a village for their garden creatures, featuring anything they can imagine: schools, soccer fields, playgrounds, stores, roads, bridges, etc.

Take a field trip to a nearby park or nature area and suggest the children bring their garden creatures. Have the children find new homes for their creatures in this environment. *How are these homes different from the garden homes?* Be sure to collect all the creatures before the group leaves!

RECOMMENDED AGES: 4⁺ ✿ OUTSIDE ✿ SPRING, SUMMER, FALL

You're Getting Warmer

DESCRIPTION

Children use ice cubes to find the warmest and coldest places in the garden. This introduces them to the concept of temperature variation and how it affects plants in their garden.

BACKGROUND

Children are often so busy playing they don't notice the temperature around them, causing adults to say, "I'm getting cold just looking at you!" This activity, best done on a warm day, focuses children's attention on finding hot and cold places in the garden, and determining which areas melt an ice cube faster or slower. By doing so, they begin to learn about the changing states of matter, while discovering that a garden is full of temperature variations.

MATERIALS

✿ 2 equal-sized ice cubes per child
✿ 1 paper cup per child
✿ (*Optional*) Tempera paint, ice cube trays, plastic wrap, ice-pop sticks

PREPARATION

Freeze the ice cubes a day before the activity, or purchase ice. It is important that all the ice cubes be very close to the same size. Just before the activity, place two ice cubes in each paper cup. *Optional:* Fill a few ice cube trays with different colors of tempera paint. Cover each tray with plastic wrap and poke ice-pop sticks through the wrap into the centers of each cube. The wrap will hold the sticks upright in the cubes while the paint freezes.

ACTIVITY

Tell the children they are going to discover the warmest and coldest parts of the garden. Invite them to guess where those places will be and discuss why they think so. Listen to their ideas about what makes a place warm or cold. You may want to record their ideas to refer back to later.

Show the children some ice cubes and ask what they know about ice. *What happens to ice when it sits out a long time? What happens to it in the freezer? What do you think will happen to it out in the garden?*

CAUTION: Children should not place their ice cubes in paths or other places where people usually walk, as this might cause someone to slip.

In the garden, ask the children to find two different places in the garden — one spot that they think will make an ice cube melt quickly, and another that will make it melt slowly. Pass out the ice cubes. Remind the children to keep their ice in their cups until they're ready to place each cube or the ice might melt in their warm hands. When they reach each spot, they can simply pour a cube out of the cup.

During the next hour, encourage the children to visit their cubes frequently. Ask, *What do you notice about the ice? Were you right about the coldest and the warmest parts of the garden?*

TYING IT TOGETHER

Have the children share where they placed their ice cubes and what happened to them. Ask, *Did anyone put their ice on the ground? Did anyone put their ice in the shade? On a white surface? On a dark surface?*

Remind the children that seeds need warmth to grow and have them think about their ice cube explorations. Ask, *Which part of the garden would be good for planting seeds? Where would you like to grow if you were a plant?*

You may want to repeat this activity at different times of day to see how the time of day affects the hottest and coldest spots in the garden.

DIGGING DEEPER

Conduct some class experiments with the children. Put ice cubes on sheets of different colored paper placed in shady and sunny spots, and on top of and underneath various surfaces. Make class predictions about what will happen. Watch and learn together.

Plant two seedlings — one in a shady spot and one in a sunny spot. Care for them equally and observe the seedlings over time with the children. Do they see any differences?

Optional: If you froze cubes of tempera paint, have the children make ice art by "painting" with the frozen cubes. This is sure to be messy, cold fun!

What's in the Box?

DESCRIPTION

Children use their sense of touch to get to know garden tools and other mystery objects. This helps children discover more about the things they might find in their garden.

BACKGROUND

Young children are often very good at paying attention to textures. They love to sift sand through their fingers, rub a cat's fur, or poke at a pinecone. In this activity they focus on their sense of touch to explore the textures of various objects in the garden and guess what they are.

MATERIALS

❋ 3 or more shoe boxes
❋ X-acto knife (for the adult only)
❋ 1 9"x6" sheet of felt for each shoe box
❋ Duct tape
❋ 3 or more objects from the garden,
  such as:
  – Seed
  – Weed
  – Flower
  – Leaf
  – Pinecone
  – Carrot
  – Trowel
  – Piece of bark
  – Small flower pot
  – Soil
  – Hose nozzle
❋ Rubber bands
❋ (*Optional*) Colorful paper to wrap boxes

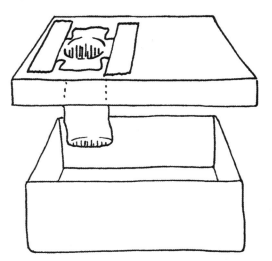

PREPARATION

In the top of each box, cut a hole just large enough for a small hand to fit through — about 3" in diameter. Create a "collar" by rolling a piece of felt into a tube with the same diameter as the hole you just cut. Tape the tube shut — it should be about 3" in diameter and 6" long. Then tape one end of the collar to the outside of the hole in the top so that when the box is closed the collar extends into the box. When children aren't watching, place a garden object or substance in each box. Close the box and put a rubber band or tape around it to keep the top on. *Optional:* Wrap each box in colorful paper, like a gift, and cut a hole in the paper around the mouth of the collar.

ACTIVITY

Gather the children in a circle and tell them they are going to learn about the garden using their sense of touch. Review with them what the sense of touch is. Ask, *Can you touch or feel with other parts of your bodies besides your fingers?* Have the children touch various items in the circle such as the carpet, the ground, their cheek, or their shoes. What words can they use to describe how the objects feel?

Explain that each box contains a garden object and the children will try to guess what the object is using only their sense of touch. Everyone will get a turn with each box. Remind them not to look in the box. When they think they know what is in the box they should whisper it to the teacher, not say it out loud.

Pass out the boxes and let the children feel their objects. After they have whispered their answers to you, have them trade boxes with each other.

TYING IT TOGETHER   When everyone has tried all the boxes, remove the objects one at a time. Ask the children to share words out loud that describe how the objects feel. Name the objects as a group and discuss their role in the garden.

DIGGING DEEPER   Go outside to the garden and invite the children to gather some new objects to put in the boxes. Let them repeat the guessing game with their parents or another group of children.

Ask the children to bring garden items from home, hidden in a bag. What do they have at home that is different from school? Set up a permanent "touch box" in the classroom and change the object regularly.

Soil Studies

The Garden Classroom

LIFE LAB, SANTA CRUZ, CA

Life Lab is a leader in garden-based education, offering field trips, summer camps, and youth internships in its Garden Classroom on the UC Santa Cruz Center for Agroecology and Sustainable Food Systems (CASFS) Farm. Drawing on decades of work with students of all ages, Life Lab has created curricula and workshops for educators interested in bringing learning to life in gardens nationwide.

Life Lab educator Juliana Grinvalsky finds that preschool-aged visitors to the Garden Classroom especially love two garden features. The Tree of Tunes is an avocado tree adorned with musical instruments made from recycled materials. "It speaks to a preschooler's kinesthetic learning style and inspires musical creativity," Juliana explains. Preschoolers also enjoy exploring and playing in Life Lab's flower tunnel, a fort-like enclosed space covered by black-eyed Susan vine (*Thunbergia*), trumpet vine, and passion flower.

Over the years, Life Lab has developed some cherished garden routines for preschool-aged children. Field trip guides have children find and care for a favorite plant during their visit. After harvesting, kids thank a plant by giving it a bit of compost or breathing some air on a leaf (plants need that carbon dioxide!). Children also always love to visit the chickens — even the rowdiest children settle down instantly to carefully cradle a baby chick in their hands. Field trip leaders also encourage kids to wander around the garden making animal noises, sporting lettuce-leaf tails or pumpkin-leaf ears.

When young children explore the garden, they can find almost anything amazing, from the feeling of a roly-poly crawling across their hands to the fun of digging in the dirt. Life Lab's field trip guides strive to look at the garden through this lens of awe, turning every small experience into a great opportunity for exploration and discovery. When designing a garden for preschool-aged children, Life Lab offers these tips:

* Choose plants with a variety of scents, textures, and leaf sizes. Encourage children to use their senses, by feeling fuzzy leaves, smelling, and even tasting with supervision.
* Mark beds and paths clearly to limit trampling, and expect some trampling anyway — if it's being used correctly, a children's garden won't be mistaken for a pristine, well-manicured place!
* Leave some beds unplanted, for digging and looking for worms.
* Scale everything appropriately — use low worm bins, build small garden beds, provide small tools and watering cans, etc.
* Include some hidey-holes, enclosed spaces, and special features, such as a plant tunnel; an outdoor "room" enclosed by trees; a big, low "nest" for group gatherings; or a Tree of Tunes.

Thousands of children explore the Garden Classroom each year, playing music under the tree, tasting fruits and vegetables straight from the source, petting chickens, holding worms, and singing songs. While Life Lab's youngest visitors may not remember the names of each plant they encounter, their visit undoubtedly plants a seed of wonder, a seed that may grow into a sense of stewardship for the earth.

RECOMMENDED AGES: 2¹/₂⁺ ❋ INSIDE/OUTSIDE ❋ ANY SEASON

Soil Exploration Station

DESCRIPTION

Children use sifters, funnels, and containers to explore the properties of sand and other soils. This activity enhances their basic knowledge of soil.

BACKGROUND

Given the opportunity to play with soils and simple tools, children soon begin experimenting with the properties of soil. They sift the soil, pour it through funnels, compact it with their hands, and notice different textures, consistencies, and particle sizes of the soils. As they uncover twigs and other objects, pack down wet soil, and feel the grittiness of sand particles, children gain an awareness of the rich variety in soils they once thought of only as "dirt." Ultimately this helps them understand that soil is the foundation of a healthy garden and that plants need it to grow well.

Set up this free exploration station indoors or outside. It is sure to be a hit with many young explorers. The key is to let children choose how and when they will experience the station's possibilities. At a station set up over an extended period of time, children have the opportunity for truly open play whenever they choose. If time is limited, you may have to more actively manage the rotation of groups through the station so that everyone who wants to has a chance to explore the soils.

MATERIALS

* ❋ 1 tub of coarse sand
* ❋ 1 tub of garden soil
* ❋ 1 tub of gravel-like, clay-like, or other soil unlike the two above (potting soil could work if you don't have a third type available)

> **CAUTION:** Fertilized soil can be toxic! Use only natural, organic soils.

* ❋ plastic tablecloth, tarp or drop cloth, broom, and dustpan (for indoor stations only)
* ❋ 3 funnels
* ❋ 3 colanders
* ❋ 3 strainers
* ❋ 3 strawberry baskets
* ❋ 3 measuring cups or plastic containers
* ❋ 3 magnifying lenses
* ❋ 3 spoons

PREPARATION

Collect the sand and soils in shallow tubs. Set up an outside station at a table or on a lawn. For an indoor station, cover a table with a plastic tablecloth, or use an empty water table. If your classroom is carpeted, cover the floor with a tarp or drop cloth. If you have hard floors, keep a broom and dustpan near the station for daily clean up.

Space the tubs as widely apart as possible to prevent children from mixing the soils. If the sand is dusty when stirred up, moisten it with water. If you don't have funnels, cut off the tops of plastic water bottles and dull the edges to create homemade, recycled funnels.

ACTIVITY

This station accommodates four to six children at a time. Introduce the station by showing the children the tubs of soil and the tools they can use to explore the soils. Demonstrate how to keep the tools in or over the tubs so the soils stay in the tubs. Ask the children why they think it might be important to keep the soil samples separate. As they explore, find out what the children notice about the different soils. Ask, *How do the soil types feel? What do they look like? Smell like? Sound like?*

TYING IT TOGETHER

Once all of the children have explored the various soils, gather around the station together to discuss how the soils are different from one another. Have the students consider these questions, using various senses: *How do the soils look different? How do they feel different? How do they sound different? How do they smell different?* Head outdoors with the children to look for new types of soil to collect for the Soil Exploration Station. Allow the children time to explore each in this same way, looking, listening, smelling, and feeling for differences.

DIGGING DEEPER

Explain that soil has to hold water for plants. Ask the children if they think some soils are better at this than other soils? Then find out! Place a few scoops of different soil types — sand, clay, potting mix — into separate strainers. Pour a small amount of water onto the soil in each strainer and see what happens. Ask, *If a soil holds water well, how might that help a plant?* Pour a large amount of water onto a soil sample and watch it come through the strainer. Explain that even good soils can only hold so much water. Apply this to lessons on how to water plants in the garden by watering a little at a time and allowing the water to soak in to the ground before adding more.

RECOMMENDED AGES: 4⁺ ❋ OUTSIDE ❋ ANY SEASON

Mud Pies

DESCRIPTION Children use their senses of hearing, sight, touch, and smell to observe how soil changes when it gets wet and when it dries out. Watching soil turn into mud and then dry out again provides an early experience with the process of evaporation.

BACKGROUND The squishy, gooey feel of mud between fingers and toes is an early sensory experience that many people remember into adulthood. Allowing children to play with mud is a wonderful way for them to experience its smells, textures, colors, and composition. Of course, this activity can get very messy, so children should dress appropriately for "Mud Day." This activity is best done on a warm, sunny day.

MATERIALS
❋ 1 to 2 buckets of soil
❋ Aluminum pie tins (one per pair of children)
❋ Ice-pop sticks or tongue depressors
❋ Trowel or other scoop for each bucket
❋ Watering can or bucket of water with cups for dipping
❋ Water

> **CAUTION:** Make sure the soil is clean and safe, and does not contain added chemicals, broken glass, or other hazards. If you're bringing in soil from an outside source, ask your local garden center to recommend something appropriate for children to play with.

PREPARATION Set up an outdoor area that can get dirty. A grassy lawn or a patio you can hose down is ideal. Put the buckets of soil in a central area. Set out the aluminum pie tins.

ACTIVITY Give each pair of children a pie tin and an ice-pop stick. Tell the children they are going to find out how soil changes. Have the pairs scoop some dry soil into their pie tins. Ask them to look at, smell, and touch the soil. Then have them listen to it by shaking it gently in the pan. Ask, *What do you think will happen to this soil when we add water?* Have the children make "pies" by mixing in a little water with an ice-pop stick until they have a thick paste. You can pour the water for the children or let them pour, in which case some students may go all the way and make soup! Any of these options is fine. Once each pair has a pie tin of mud, let them decorate their pies with flower petals, sand, sticks, and stones from around the garden. When the pies are done, set them in a sunny spot to "cook." Ask, *What do you think will happen to our pies?*

TYING IT TOGETHER Check the pies for "doneness" over the next few hours or days. How fast they dry out will

depend on the temperature and humidity in your area. Once the pies are dry, challenge the children to turn them back into mud, or break them up into cookies. Have the students visit and observe their pies over weeks and months. Ask, *What's happening to our pies? Where do you think the water is going?* The easiest way to clean up Mud Pies is to allow them to dry completely, and then push them out of the tins and onto a compost pile or patch of soil.

DIGGING DEEPER

For wonderfully messy group fun, have the children dump their dry dirt on an old tarp, ask an adult to add water from a watering can, and let the children mix the mud with their feet!

To learn more about soils, make "mudshakes." Put a few cups of garden soil in a jar with a lid (a large plastic mayonnaise jar works well) and add water almost to the top of the jar. Have the children take turns shaking the jar to mix up the mudshake, then let the jar sit for several hours while the soil settles. Without moving the jar, encourage the children to watch how the soil settles. What do they notice? What happens when they try this with different types of soil? Depending on the size of the soil particles, the soil will settle into layers — basically of sand, silt, clay, and organic matter — with the largest particles of sand sinking to the bottom; the particles of silt in the middle; and the smallest particles of clay near the top and sometimes remaining suspended in cloudy water for a long time.

Engage children in a discussion about where soil comes from and how it is formed. What are their ideas? Their conceptions may surprise you! Read *The Sun, the Wind, and the Rain* by Lisa Peters to give them some more ideas.

RECOMMENDED AGES: 2$^1/_2$+ ❋ OUTSIDE ❋ FALL

Pumpkin Decomposition Experiment

DESCRIPTION

Children predict and observe what happens when they leave two pumpkins outside. This activity gives students an opportunity to observe and study decomposition, one of the most important processes in the garden and in nature.

BACKGROUND

Decomposition, or decay, is the process by which fungus, bacteria, and invertebrates change once-living matter — such as fallen leaves, rotting logs, and the like — into fertile soil. Decomposition is not just a necessary process in the garden, but a crucial part of the life cycle. It's an immeasurably important concept in ecology, and the garden provides us with a wonderful place to witness decomposition first hand.

Decomposition is a concept that children will become more acquainted with as they age. What's most important to relay to young children is that dead material helps grow new life in our garden. As they watch a pumpkin rot, they'll see beetles, worms, mold, and other tiny organisms participating in this cycle! In addition to those they see, there are millions of microorganisms too small to see, which are all aiding in the process.

MATERIALS

❋ One uncarved pumpkin
❋ One carved pumpkin
❋ (Optional) Wood and paints for a garden experiment sign
❋ (Optional) Camera
❋ Hand lenses
❋ (Optional) *Pumpkin Pumpkin* by Jean Titherington and/or *Pumpkin Circle: The Story of a Garden* by George Levenson

PREPARATION

Locate a protected spot near your classroom where you can leave your pumpkins to decompose on a patch of soil or under a bush. You probably need to get permission from the grounds keeping staff and you may want put up a sign by the pumpkins explaining your experiment so that it doesn't get cleaned up.

ACTIVITY

Ask, *What do you think will happen if we leave our pumpkins outside?* Record the children's ideas and then together place your pumpkins in their outside spot. Take a picture if possible. Ask the children to describe what the pumpkins look like now, and record their answers.

Visit the pumpkins every day or at least twice a week. During this time, you can also read pumpkin stories aloud, starting with *Pumpkin Pumpkin* and later, near the end of your

experiment, *Pumpkin Circle*. Each time you visit, ask the children to describe the appearance of the pumpkins and what is happening to them, and record their observations with pictures or words. Take another photograph. Using their hand lenses, have students search for worms, beetles, and other decomposers at work and discuss their role in munching up the pumpkins and helping turn them back into soil. Be sure to have the children look for mold and fungus as well!

TYING IT TOGETHER

When the pumpkins are gone or mostly gone, continue to visit the spot and see if new plants begin to grow there. Review the predictions the class made about what might happen to the pumpkins. Display your photographs and read the children's observations about the pumpkins over time. Ask, *What happened to our pumpkins? Why? What helped the pumpkins break down? What would happen if things didn't break down like this?*

Decomposition is a concept that is easy to reiterate on a frequent basis in the garden. Situations constantly arise where you can ask children things like, *What would happen to this tomato if we left it here on the ground? I don't want my apple core; who might eat it for me?* Keep this concept in the back of your mind and remind students periodically of the life cycles
taking place in your garden.

DIGGING DEEPER

As you begin the experiment, place another object — a pile of wet leaves, another variety of fruit or vegetable, or a piece of plastic or styrofoam — next to the pumpkins and compare what happens to it. *Which object decomposes more quickly? Which has more bugs and other decomposers on it?* Watch and learn together.

Play pumpkin leapfrog! Place four to eight pumpkins a few feet apart in the garden and have students hop over each one. Then try pumpkin slalom, where children run in an S-figure through a line of pumpkins.

Have a pumpkin seed tasting. Roast pumpkin seeds from a carved pumpkin or buy some in the store. Taste and compare seeds prepared in a variety of ways, such as roasted seeds, toasted seeds, salted seeds, and unsalted seeds.

RECOMMENDED AGES: 2+ ✾ INSIDE/OUTSIDE ✾ ANY SEASON (INSIDE IN COLD AREAS)

A Home for Worms

DESCRIPTION

Creating a worm habitat is an excellent way to recycle food scraps from your classroom. A worm habitat is also a great place for children to observe and explore the wonder of worms.

BACKGROUND

Using worms to compost, or vermicomposting, is a great addition to any outdoor classroom. In a vermicomposting system, decomposition is performed by a type of worm called a red wiggler. Worms eat decaying material and turn it into worm castings, a nutrient-rich organic material that plants love. These worms are capable of eating from 50 percent to 100 percent of their weight in kitchen scraps each day. Students can watch food scraps turn into castings over a period of just a few months. When maintained properly, a worm habitat does not smell bad or cause any problems. Worm habitats work just as well indoors as outdoors, and the worms double as classroom pets! For more information about vermicomposting, see Let Worms Make Your Compost (p. 108).

MATERIALS

✾ Empty worm bin
✾ Bedding material (damp, shredded newspaper or cardboard; hay; coconut pith, etc.)
✾ 1 lb red wiggler worms
✾ Spray bottle
✾ Kitchen scraps
✾ (Optional) Burlap sack

PREPARATION

You will need to build a worm bin (see p. 117) or purchase one for this activity. The National Gardening Association offers a number of options at *www. gardeningwithkids.org.*

Gather bedding, making sure to use chemical-free material. Pesticides, herbicides, and fertilizers will kill the worms and aren't safe for a children's activity. If you're using newspaper, choose papers without heavy dyes or gloss. The best choice may be to combine two or three types of bedding material.

Collect one pound of red wiggler worms. Red wigglers are not the earthworms your students will find in your garden soil. Red wigglers are a hardier species of worm that can live in warmer indoor temperatures as well as in the shallow layer of bedding material in your worm habitat. Red wigglers are sold by the pound. You can collect and use worms from someone else's active worm habitat, buy them locally (check at an area nursery), or purchase them online from the National Gardening Association (*www.gardeningwithkids.org*).

ACTIVITY

Lay out the bedding materials for your worm bin and show the kids the red wigglers. Explain that the worms need a home and the children are going to help you build it. Depending on how many children are in the class, you might need to divide them into pairs or small groups and assign each a separate task.

Explain to the children that worms need something to crawl through in their home and this will be your bedding material. Have each group add several handfuls of bedding to the bin, filling it most of the way. If you're using newspaper, show the children how to shred it into strips. Next, using a spray bottle, have one group dampen the bedding with water. Monitor this step carefully. The bedding should about as moist as a wrung-out sponge.

The habitat is now ready for its guests! Put a red wiggler and some soil in your hand and have the children describe the worm to you. Ask, *Why do you think they call these worms red wigglers?* A healthy, deep-red worm should give the answer away! Let children hold a worm if they'd like to, making sure they also have some dirt in their hands. The dirt helps the worms to retain their body moisture. Have children add all the red wigglers to the bin.

Worms need some time to settle in. After a week, it is time to add food. You can add about one quart of food every two to three days. Feeding appropriate kitchen scraps to your worms is very important. Worms don't do well with a lot of citrus, anything oily, or scraps with high water content. Never feed worms meat or dairy products. In addition to the obvious plant-based food scraps, such as banana peels, bread slices, and apple cores, your worms will also eat coffee grounds, eggshells, tea bags and shredded paper products, such as egg cartons. The smaller the scraps, the sooner they start to rot and the faster the worms can eat them.

After the children feed their worms, they should always cover the new food with more bedding to protect the worms. You can also lay a burlap sack over the top of the food and bedding. It will protect the worms and create a fun opportunity for the children to "tuck in" their worms.

Worms prefer a consistent moisture level in their home — the contents of your worm bin should always be as moist as a wrung-out sponge. Get your class on a regular watering cycle for the worm bin. At first, check the dampness of the bedding material frequently and keep track of how often and how much water you add.

TYING IT TOGETHER

As your worm bin matures, have the children explore it for organisms other than worms. The students should find some bugs they didn't add, such as pill bugs, springtails, or pot worms. Ask, *How do you think these visitors got in? Do you think there might be living things in this bin that we can't see with our eyes?*

Have your students compost leftovers from their lunches on a regular basis. Add "compost" to their regular routine of separating trash from recycling. At the end of every snack or lunch period, review the leftover scraps. Ask, *Would our worms think this plastic bag is yummy? What about this banana peel?* Give positive reinforcement for the love and care the children show for their pet worms. *Perhaps the worms will thank us with castings for our garden!*

DIGGING DEEPER

Try feeding your worms different sizes and types of scraps and compare how quickly they are eaten. *Do worms prefer one kind of food over another?* Ask children to think about why some scraps may have been left behind. *If these scraps are larger than other scraps, could they be taking longer to decompose? Were they added to the bin recently? Maybe worms don't like egg shells as much as they like coffee grounds!* Encourage children to speculate and ponder.

Be sure to involve your students in harvesting your worm castings (next activity)!

RECOMMENDED AGES: 3+ ✿ INSIDE/OUTSIDE ✿ ANY SEASON

Harvesting Worm Castings

DESCRIPTION   Children harvest worm castings from their worm bin and put the castings on their garden beds. They see what their worms create, help make the garden soil healthier, and choose the types of beneficial organisms they want to keep in their bin. This activity is a perfect follow-up to A Home for Worms (p. 41).

BACKGROUND   Do this activity a few months after your class has established its worm bin (p. 41). Over time, the worm bin becomes full of moist, dark, earthy material. That's your worm poop, or castings. These castings are safe for students to touch and they are odor-free. Harvesting the castings may be the best part of having a worm bin, and is a fun class activity that brings your worm investigations full circle.

MATERIALS
✿ Two small buckets
✿ Damp soil
✿ Sheets of newspaper or a tarp
✿ Matured worm bin
✿ Bedding material (damp, shredded newspaper or cardboard; hay; coconut pith, etc.)

PREPARATION   Fill the small buckets with damp soil. Worms are highly sensitive to heat, so be sure the children's hands have moist soil on them whenever they handle worms, such as during harvesting. Keep the buckets nearby for children to dip their hands in throughout the activity.

Spread a thick layer of newspapers, or a tarp, over a large area of ground.

ACTIVITY   Enlist the help of a parent or some older children and split the children into groups of three to five students. Have the first group help you gently transfer the contents of the worm bin onto the newspaper or tarp. Immediately fill the bottom of your emptied bin with new bedding.

With dirt-covered hands, have students carefully remove the worms from the worm castings, placing the worms and any remaining food scraps on the new bedding in the worm bin. Ask, *Are there any other creatures in our castings that we'd like to keep in our bin?* The children might want to move some of the pill bugs and pot worms back to the worm habitat. If they look very closely at the bits of worm castings stuck to the worms, the children should see that they're tossing springtails back into the bin as well.

Ask, *What's left on the newspaper or tarp, now that you've returned all the worms and food scraps to the bin?* Worm castings! Explain to the children that the castings they've just harvested are a plant's favorite food. Ask them where they'd like to put the castings in the garden. Do the plants in one bed seem to need them more than another? If the plants in all beds are equally healthy, spread the castings evenly on all the beds. You may also choose to add the castings to a bed you are just about to plant, giving the seeds or baby plants lots of food to help them grow. Your students will take pride in knowing that they helped make the soil healthier just by taking care of their worms!

TYING IT TOGETHER

If you have a standing compost pile, encourage the children to explore that finished compost. Have them hold a handful of it next to a handful of worm castings. Ask, *How are they similar? How are they different?* Consider setting up a Soil Exploration Station (p. 35) to compare compost, worm castings, and organic potting soil.

DIGGING DEEPER

Ask the children to imagine being worms that eat rotting food and garbage. As a class, create a menu — breakfast, lunch, and dinner — of the kind of garbage they'd eat in a day. Using the menu, have the children write or tell a story about A Day in the Life of a Worm in their worm bin. They can add their own illustrations and keep the story next to their worm bin.

Growing Activities

Sunflower Kids

SANTA CRUZ, CA

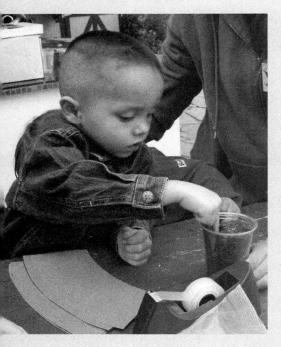

Janine Canada has taught garden-based early childhood education (ECE) for more than 25 years. Early on, she ran an intergenerational program, using the garden at a nearby seniors' center. More recently, she started Sunflower Kids, a garden-based childcare center run out of her home. Gardens have featured prominently in all of Janine's ECE programs, making her an expert on teaching and managing young children in the garden, and she is active in sharing her passion for gardening with young children and other early childhood educators. Following the death of her beloved golden retriever, Janine wrote and published *Gardening with Gus*, a book of ECE garden activities based on her years of nurturing children's connection to the garden and the natural world around them.

A garden is a distinctive learning environment requiring unique rules and expectations. Janine recommends having just a few rules and reviewing them with students at the start of garden activities. "Morning circle time is our place to talk about garden rules, but we don't have many — the children are naturally respectful of the garden," she says.

Fun garden tasks are an important activity in the Sunflower Kids garden. Janine has pictures of garden tasks, such as raking, hoeing, filling the bird feeder, refreshing the birdbath, watering the garden, feeding the animals and giving food scraps to the worms, and — when he was alive — brushing Gus. As the children arrive every day, they choose a task and Janine posts the picture of that task next to the child's name. At lunchtime, Janine writes down each child's morning activities so parents know what their children have been up to that day.

Janine was moved by Gus's patience with the children. He helped them learn about pets and become more connected with the garden, and she recommends a dog or other pet to any teacher for whom it's a practical possibility. The Sunflower Kids also take care of goldfish and a rabbit — and, of course, their worms.

The children love to harvest fruits and vegetables from the garden and participate in cooking projects. Some of their favorites include making zucchini bread, applesauce, and fresh pesto from their garden basil. One summer the children had a fresh lemonade stand and "sold" cups of the tasty brew along with freshly baked cookies to their parents and neighbors. Janine incorporates various learning concepts such as counting, sorting, measuring, writing, art, cooperation, sharing, and following directions in all the activities.

When asked about lessons to share with other teachers, Janine offers this advice. "Let the kids lead. Ask lots of questions about everything. You may not always get the replies you anticipate, but instead responses you'd never have considered." As students ask questions and seek answers through their own explorations and observations, they become active leaders in their own outdoor education.

RECOMMENDED AGES: 4+ ❋ INSIDE/OUTSIDE ❋ ANY SEASON

Bean Babies

DESCRIPTION

Children watch seeds sprout in bags hung around their necks. These seeds will be used for exploration in the following activity, Seed Secrets.

BACKGROUND

Seeds are one way a plant makes more of itself. Starting flowers and vegetables from seed is an inexpensive and fun way to grow a garden. You can save some seeds from your current garden to plant next year. You can also purchase seeds at a garden center or order them from catalogs.

Seeds come in many shapes, sizes, and colors. No matter what they look like, all seeds have the same basic parts: a seed coat to protect the seed; an embryo that is the baby plant; and stored food called endosperm that feeds the embryo until it becomes a seedling and can make its own food.

As seeds dry out on a plant, the baby plants inside the seeds stop growing. To grow again (germinate), a seed needs water and warmth. Water makes the seed swell up and burst the seed coat. The tiny first root then pushes through and reaches down into the soil, while the shoot pushes upward towards the light. The seed leaves, or cotyledons, carry the seed's stored food supply. By carefully taking apart the seeds they've sprouted in their necklaces (which they will do in the Seed Secrets activity), students can observe all these parts.

MATERIALS

❋ Hole punch
❋ 1 small plastic jewelry bag per child (found at local bead or craft stores)
❋ String
❋ Masking tape
❋ Variety of large seeds (fava, pinto, kidney, or scarlet runner beans, etc.) — enough for three to four seeds per child
❋ Bowls
❋ Cotton balls
❋ Water

PREPARATION

Punch a hole in the top of each jewelry bag and run a long piece of string through it. Use tape to label each necklace with a child's name. Set aside three of each type of dry seed to compare with the soaked seeds later on. Place the remaining seeds in bowls.

Create an "assembly line," with a bowl of ready-made necklaces, a bowl of cotton balls, a bowl of water, and the bowls of seeds.

ACTIVITY

Lead the children in a short discussion about seeds and plants. Ask, *What grows from a seed? What does a seed need in order to grow into a plant (soil, sun, water, air)?* Explain that some seeds land on soil and, with some warmth from the sun and moisture from the rain, grow into a plant. Other seeds, like the ones in front of them, need all of those things, and also a fifth ingredient: care. *Some seeds need the love and care of a gardener in order to turn into a plant, and that's where you come in.* In this activity, the children provide that fifth ingredient by wearing the seeds around their necks and watching a baby plant, or sprout, start to grow.

Show students the assembly line. Demonstrate how to create a Bean Baby by picking up a necklace, taking a cotton ball, dipping it in water, squeezing out any excess water, and placing it inside the baggie on the necklace. Then choose a few seeds, place them in the bag, seal the bag, and hang the necklace around your neck. Explain that the cotton serves as the "soil" for their seeds in this experiment. To grow into a full plant, however, the seedlings need to be planted in real soil.

Now pass out each child's ready-made necklace. Have the children move along the assembly line repeating the steps you showed them, and ending up with three or four Bean Babies in each necklace.

Explain that not only are the children giving the seeds love, but with their body heat, they are also keeping the seeds warm. At night, the seeds can stay at school and wait to be worn when the children come back.

Consider doing this activity on a Friday so that, on Monday, children will return to find a dramatic change has taken place in their seeds. However, remember that those seeds need warmth when the children are away, so hang them in a window over the weekend.

TYING IT TOGETHER

Invite students to describe what they think their seeds will look like in a few days. Illustrate what they describe on a large piece of paper, adding features each time a child shares a new prediction.

Check the seeds every day, comparing what the children see with their original predictions. Give the children the opportunity to revise their predictions based on their daily observations.

DIGGING DEEPER

Plant the same types of seeds you used for this activity in soil so the children can watch the seeds grow into full-sized plants (see the Container Seeds activity for information on how to do this.)

After a few days, plan on doing the Seed Secrets activity with your students. This involves looking at a variety of dry seeds, then dissecting sprouted seeds from the children's necklaces.

RECOMMENDED AGES: 2¹/₂⁺ ❋ INSIDE/OUTSIDE ❋ ANY SEASON

Seed Secrets

DESCRIPTION Children explore a variety of seeds and make observations, then dissect seeds to find out what's inside. Discovering the parts of a seed helps them better understand how new plants are born. It's fun to follow this activity with Six Seed Trail Mix (p. 81).

BACKGROUND See the background for Bean Babies (p. 47).

MATERIALS
* ❋ A bowl of large, dry beans to dissect (fava, pinto, kidney, and scarlet runner beans all work well), *or* students' soaked seeds from Bean Babies
* ❋ 3 dry seed samples of the same kind for comparison
* ❋ Tarp or oil cloth
* ❋ A tub or water table to set up a seed exploration station
* ❋ A variety of seeds — enough to fill your tub or water table: Include edible seeds from your kitchen, such as assorted beans, nuts, and grains, and seeds from your garden or packaged seeds (for fun, include a coconut to show one of the biggest seeds)
* ❋ Tools for exploring seeds: spoons, funnels, film canisters, magnifying glasses, cups of different sizes, etc.
* ❋ Hand lenses

PREPARATION Before doing the activity, soak all but three of the large bean seeds overnight. If you made Bean Babies with your students, you can use the seeds from students' necklaces. Take out one 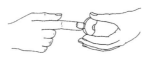 soaked seed ahead of time and pry it open with your fingers, splitting it in half along the seem. If it opens easily, your seeds are ready. Otherwise, continue soaking until they are ready.

Lay down a tarp or oil cloth and place the tub or water table on it. Pour the various dry seeds into the tub or water table to create a seed exploration station. Place the exploration tools (spoons, funnels, etc.) on top of the seeds.

ACTIVITY Do this activity in small groups or as an exploration station. Let children play with and explore the dry seeds using the tools in the tub and their sense of touch. Ask, *What do you notice about the seeds?* Offer hand lenses and see if the children discover anything they hadn't noticed before. Encourage children to sort them into different categories. Ask, *Which ones are shiny? Round? Striped? Pointy? Colorful? Can you make a design with them? Which one do you think will sprout the fastest? Which do you think comes from the biggest plant? The smallest? What kinds of plants do you think the seeds might turn into? What will the flowers look like? Can you think of a way to find out?* Encourage the children to ask you questions about the seeds, too.

After you have finished observing the seeds, draw the children's attention to their sprouted seeds. Take a seed out of the water or from a necklace, and set it on a piece of paper. Place one of the dry seeds you reserved next to it. Look closely at the two beans: wet and dry. *How did the water affect the beans? How do the soaked beans look and feel different from the dried beans?* (The soaking causes the seed coat to loosen — the seed is beginning to grow!)

Using your two thumbnails, gently pry a bean open along its larger edge. Separate the halves and show the children the tiny embryo. Ask, *What do you see?* (A baby plant, waiting to grow!) Invite students to split their own seeds, with help as needed. Show them how to use magnifying glasses to look closely at the baby plants inside.

TYING IT TOGETHER

Gather the children and ask, *What seeds do we eat?* (Remember that wheat, corn, beans, rice, and nuts are seeds.) *Why are seeds so nutritious?* Life comes from seeds! A whole plant grows from a seed.

DIGGING DEEPER

Help children role play what it might be like to be a seed planted in the ground and starting to grow. Have them S-T-R-E-T-C-H their toes (roots) down into the soil and R-E-A-C-H their arms (seed leaves) up towards the light. Try to imagine the feel of rain, sun, and wind on the growing plant.

CAUTION: Before making seed snacks, check with parents to be sure no children are allergic to any of your proposed ingredients!

Make a seed snack — for example, crackers (ground wheat seeds) with peanut butter (ground peanut seeds), or corn chips (ground corn seeds) with hummus (ground garbanzo bean seeds).

If there are any sprouted, but undissected seeds left over, consider planting them so the children can watch their seeds grow! (See Seed Starting and Transplanting, p. 95, for planting directions.)

Catching Hitchhikers

DESCRIPTION

Children explore the variety of ways that plants spread their seeds by pulling on an extra sock and walking through a field. Then they examine their socks to see what seeds are sticking to them, and finally, they plant their socks to find out what grows.

BACKGROUND

Have you ever wondered how a plant gets to where it's growing? Seeds are transported in a variety of ways. Some are light and have wings so that the wind can carry them away. Some seeds are able to float in the ocean for many days, land on a beach and sprout in the sand. Others are packaged in a sweet, brightly colored fruit, so that animals will eat them and pass them through their bodies and back into the soil. Still others have barbs or other velcro-like parts that hook onto animals' fur to travel to a new location. These seeds also stick to our clothing.

MATERIALS

❊ Large adult socks, preferably white (one per child)
❊ Milk cartons split lengthwise, 1-gallon pots, or other containers for planting (one per child)
❊ Organic potting soil
❊ Watering can
❊ Magnifying lenses

PREPARATION

The best time to pick up seeds on your socks is summer or fall. Scout some good spots for seed collecting — a meadow or grassy lot often features weeds with seeds that will brush off onto socks. Walk through the meadow with socks on to be sure this spot has seeds that will stick to socks.

ACTIVITY

Ask, *How do seeds spread to new places to grow new plants?* Tell the children they're going to find out about one way seeds spread: by sticking to things and hitching a ride. Give each child a sock that fits over his or her shoe and help him or her pull it on. Lead the group on a walk through a garden, field, or wooded area. Ask, *Do you see any seeds trying to hitch a ride?*

After the walk, have the children sit down, carefully remove their socks, and look closely to see if anything is sticking to the socks. Ask them to take turns sharing what they find. Offer hand lenses and see if the children discover anything they hadn't noticed before. *Can you see how the seeds stick to your socks? Do the seeds have hooks? What else do you notice about these seeds?*

When the children are finished looking for seeds, help each child fill a pot about 3/4 full with potting soil and lay his or her sock on top of the soil. Have them cover their socks with a *thin* layer of soil and gently press the soil down. Weed seeds can't be buried too deeply or they will not sprout. Water the pots and keep the soil moist until the seeds sprout.

TYING IT TOGETHER

Where did these seeds come from? Why do you think they stuck to our socks? What else might walk through the meadow that seeds might stick to?

What do you think will happen now that we have planted the seeds? Does anyone have guesses about what the new plants will look like? Will those new plants have seeds?

DIGGING DEEPER

Have the children draw a picture of their seedy socks and then draw pictures of their "sock

Seed illustrations courtesy of the National Gardening Association

RECOMMENDED AGES: 2⁺ ❋ INSIDE/OUTSIDE ❋ SPRING, SUMMER, FALL

Container Seeds

DESCRIPTION Children fill cups, six packs, or other containers with soil and learn the basics of how to plant seeds and take care of young seedlings.

BACKGROUND You can sow seeds directly in the ground, or start them in containers and transplant the seedlings into the garden later. Consult the Vegetable Planting Guide (p. 98) or the information on the back of the seed packet to determine which technique to use for which seeds. For example, carrots, beets, and other root vegetables are best sown directly in the garden — their roots don't transplant well. On the other hand, many fruiting vegetables (e.g., tomatoes and peppers) grow best when started in containers.

Many people start seeds in containers to get a jump on spring. You can grow seedlings indoors under lights and later, after all danger of frost, plant the healthiest ones in the garden. Planting indoors in containers allows you to look after small seedlings until they get big and strong enough to fend for themselves in the garden. You can protect them indoors from insects, birds, slugs, stray footsteps, cold weather, floods, and drought. (See Seed Starting and Transplanting, p. 95, for more seed-starting information.)

Use your imagination when choosing containers; you can use small pots, cut-off milk cartons, yogurt containers, or old six-pack plant containers. Just make sure to poke holes in the bottom of any container you use, so that water can drain out.

When considering which vegetables to grow in a preschool garden, think about palatability as well as steps to preparation. Bite-sized vegetables — cherry tomatoes, string beans, peas — are ideal because kids usually like them and they can pick and eat these vegetables with no processing needed. Cucumbers, carrots, lettuce, bell peppers, broccoli, and celery can all be eaten raw with minimal preparation; on the other hand, vegetables like eggplant or potatoes take more work.

MATERIALS
* ❋ 3 or more 2"- to 4"-deep containers per child (you can use anything that will hold soil and has or can have holes punched in the bottom)
* ❋ Commercial, organic seed-starting mix or your own mix (made from 5 parts compost, 4 parts garden soil, and 1 part sand)
* ❋ Watering can, hose with a mist nozzle, or spray bottle
* ❋ Seeds (enough for 3–4 per container)
* ❋ Small plant labels (use ice-pop sticks, or cut out labels from old plastic containers)
* ❋ Pencil or indelible pen
* ❋ (*Optional*) Row cover or netting from a garden store (to protect outside seedlings from birds)

PREPARATION Poke holes in the container bottoms, if necessary. Prepare a workspace — outside or inside — on a surface lined with newspapers. Set out a large container of seed-starting mix.

ACTIVITY   Show children how to fill their containers with seed-starting mix, holding the containers directly over the larger container of seed-starting mix to prevent a mess. Have students carefully tap the containers on the ground to remove air pockets, and then add more soil to fill the containers to within 1/2 inch of the top. Moisten the soil mixture in the containers with a gentle spray until it is wet but not soggy.

Demonstrate the "drill" method of planting, one step at a time. First, show the children how to lay 3 or 4 seeds on the soil surface (using multiple seeds should guarantee that at least one seed per container germinates, helping everyone to have a successful experience). Have an adult help the children do this and then show them how to carefully poke the seeds into the mix, one by one, and cover them with soil. The seed packet will indicate how deep to plant the seeds. The general rule is to plant seeds to a depth twice the size of the seed. Make sure the seeds don't get poked too deep, because the sprouts may not make it to the surface.

> **Tip:** Teach children to "drill" to a specific point on their finger, such as their fingernail or knuckle.

Help the children label their containers. Explain that we do this to remember what we planted and, in this case, also to remember who each container belongs to. Ask, *What should we put on each label?* Here are some possibilities:

- The type of flower or vegetable
- The date you planted it
- The child's name
- A good-luck message for your seed! (Some children enjoy putting this message on the part of the label that goes underground, since that's where the seed is.)

Place the containers in a warm place and be sure the soil never dries out. Water the seeds as needed using a gentle spray, but be careful! Soggy soil is often the cause for seed failure. Aim to keep the soil about as moist as a wrung-out sponge. Once the seeds sprout, make sure they get at least eight hours of light each day. A sunny window works well, or you can use fluorescent lights positioned a few inches above the seedlings (adjust the height of the lights as the seedlings grow). If all danger of frost has passed, you can set the containers of baby seedlings on a table outside. In this case, be sure to cover them with a net so hungry birds don't eat the new shoots. Transplant the seedlings when they are about 4 inches tall and have two sets of leaves (see the next activity, Setting Out Seedlings, p. 55).

> **Tip:** Keep your seed packets. They provide important information about how to grow the seeds inside. If a particular variety grows really well, you will want to remember what it was so you can plant it again next year. Some people laminate empty seed packets and use them as plant labels.

TYING IT TOGETHER   Have a discussion about germination and plant growth. Ask, *How will our containers look when the seeds begin to grow? Which seeds do you think will sprout first?* Once the seeds sprout ask, *How do the seedlings look similar? How do they look different? Do seeds all sprout at the same time? How long do you think the seedlings will be happy in this container?*

DIGGING DEEPER   When you transplant the seedlings into their permanent places in the garden, it's important to space them according to the seed packet directions. Why is this spacing important? Here's a fun way to find out. Fill three 4" pots with potting soil. Plant 2 radish seeds in the first pot,

5 radish seeds in the second pot, and 20 radish seeds in the third. Keep the soil moist and observe what happens. After a few weeks you should have some radishes to sample. Before harvesting them ask, *How do the plants in each pot look?* After you harvest, draw the children's attention to the roots in each container. Ask, *What differences do you notice about the radishes in each pot? Which seed spacing grew the best radishes?*

Help the children create "Seed Nuggets" by rolling balls of clay in wildflower seeds and allowing them to dry. Head out to an open area in the garden and toss the Seed Nuggets. Water and watch what emerges!

RECOMMENDED AGES: 4+ ❀ OUTSIDE ❀ SPRING, SUMMER, FALL

Setting Out Seedlings

DESCRIPTION

Children plant a garden bed with the seedlings they started in Container Seeds (p. 52), or store-bought seedlings. During this activity, students gain experience in transplanting seedlings into the ground.

BACKGROUND

When seedlings have developed their second set of true leaves, it's time to transplant them into the garden. They have outgrown their containers and now need room to spread out and take off.

Young seedlings must be handled very gently to avoid damaging the plant parts. Once you've removed the seedlings from their flat or container it is important to get them in the ground as soon as possible. If you can, choose a cloudy or rainy day for setting out seedlings to avoid shock to the young plants. Otherwise, try to plant in the evening or early morning hours. Water the seedlings thoroughly before transplanting so the plants' cells are full of water.

How you space seedlings depends on the size of the mature plant. In general, the leaves of the mature plants should just touch each other. Check the seed packet or seedling label for directions.

MATERIALS

❀ Seedlings ready for transplant (from the previous activity or a nursery)
❀ Trowels
❀ A prepared garden bed

PREPARATION

If your seedlings have been growing indoors, they need to be "hardened off" before you transplant them outdoors. Starting about a week before transplanting, bring the seedlings outside to a sheltered spot. Start by leaving them outside for a few hours and extend the period each day. Meanwhile, prepare one or more garden bed(s) for planting. (See Preparing In-Ground Garden Beds, p. 93.)

ACTIVITY

Because seedlings must be handled with care, planting them requires quite a bit of adult participation. Involve the children in planning where each plant should grow. *Tomatoes are the biggest plants we're planting; where should they go? Marigolds keep pests away, so shall we plant them in between our other plants?* Help students use a hand trowel to mark out where each plant will go prior to planting.

Show children how to dig a hole (with hands or a trowel) that is bigger than the root ball of their plant. Have them dig a hole for each seedling before you remove it from the container, to avoid drying out the roots from too much exposure to sun and air.

Gently remove a seedling from its container by holding the container upside down with one hand over the container opening, and pinching the sides of the container to coax out the plant and soil. On a 6-pack, use your thumb to gently push each plant out of its cell. Keep as much soil around the roots as possible.

Have an adult lower the seedling into place and hold it there while the children fill the hole around it with soil and gently pat down the soil around the stem. Encourage children to be gentle by demonstrating how to carefully "tuck in" their seedlings. Younger children often enjoy blowing a kiss to each seedling for good luck.

Water the plants right away, and label them. A great way to involve children in watering is to provide one big bucket of water with many small cups. Have the children fill their cup, walk it over to their plant and pour, and then return for more water if needed. This gives each student a chance to participate in watering, and helps to prevent any one student from overwatering, as often happens if they use a watering can or hose. Remember to have an adult supervisor by the bucket of water at all times, and empty the bucket when you leave the garden.

Tip: You can protect young seedlings from hungry birds by placing a net supported by stakes over the whole bed. Inquire at a garden center about netting or "row cover."

While children will enjoy helping to keep the plants watered, keeping all the plants healthy and thoroughly watered will require time and work beyond the time your students spend watering. For general Watering Tips, see p. 97.

TYING IT TOGETHER

Have a discussion with the children about basic plant needs. Ask, *How can we take care of this garden we created? What does it need from us? What will we get from this garden if all goes well?*

Take a picture of your children with their new garden after planting. Take another picture every two weeks or so to track the progress of the garden.

DIGGING DEEPER

Long ago people in Europe began the practice of creating "knot gardens," intricate designs made up of low-growing plants. You can create your own knot garden by first outlining your design on the soil with powdered lime or light-colored sand, and then planting your seedlings along the lines. Remember to think about the size of the mature plants and space accordingly!

RECOMMENDED AGES: 2+   ✿   OUTSIDE   ✿   SPRING, SUMMER, FALL

Garden in a Box

DESCRIPTION   Children plant seeds outdoors in a container. This activity can demonstrate that gardens come in many shapes and sizes!

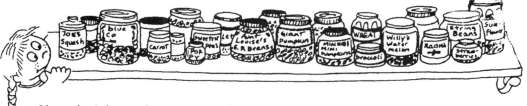

BACKGROUND   If you don't have a large, in-ground garden site, you can grow a bountiful harvest of herbs, vegetables, and flowers in small raised beds or containers filled with soil. If you're gardening in containers, place them in a sunny spot such as a balcony or patio, and choose plant varieties that are suited to growing in small spaces.

Use six-inch-deep containers to grow leaf vegetables and herbs, and 12-inch-deep ones to grow fruiting plants like tomatoes or peppers. You can use a wide variety of recycled materials as creative planting pots. Examples include: fruit crates, wine barrels, cement blocks, buckets, trash cans, old baskets, and Styrofoam coolers. Line baskets and fruit crates with plastic trash bags and, if necessary, punch drainage holes in the bottom of the container and liner.

Choose plants carefully. Think about how big the mature plants will be when deciding how many seeds to sow in each container. Also consider how many plants of a certain type you will need to ensure that each child gets a taste. For example, you might want to plant plenty of carrots for class carrot snacks, but only six lettuce plants for class salads. Brighten the mix with an edible flower like a miniature cascading nasturtium.

MATERIALS
* Planting containers
* Plastic bags to line the containers (if needed)
* Homemade or commercial organic potting soil (to make your own, mix 5 parts compost with 4 parts topsoil and 1 part sand)
* Seeds for plants that thrive when sown directly in the garden (carrots, beets, beans, lettuce, nasturtiums, etc.)
* Trowels, old cream cheese tubs, or yogurt containers for scooping soil
* (*Optional*) Camera

> **CAUTION:** Be sure to use unfertilized soil. Read the label and avoid bags with the phrase, "Keep away from children."

PREPARATION   Involve the children ahead of time in planning your container garden. Ask, *Can we grow plants even if we don't have a garden bed in the ground? How might we grow vegetables and flowers? What could we use as planters?* Together, brainstorm, collect, and prepare recycled materials to use as planting containers. Then scout out a safe spot for your plants that receives at least six hours of sun daily. On planting day, ask parents to dress their children in clothes that can get dirty. Set any large containers in their permanent locations before you fill and plant them, so you don't have to move heavy containers of soil. Line the containers with plastic bags if necessary. Finally, fill all containers with organic potting soil.

ACTIVITY   Once your containers are full, it's time to plant. There are three techniques for planting seeds in large containers:

Drilling is appropriate for planting large seeds like peas or sunflowers, and is the easiest method for young children. Place the seeds on the surface of the soil, spacing them appropriately. Then push each seed into the soil to its correct depth (about 2x its width) and cover with soil.

Furrowing works well for mid-sized seeds, such as beets or radishes. Show children how to use their finger or a stick to make a furrow, or shallow ditch, the length of the container and the depth the seed should be planted. Drop the seeds into the furrow, spacing them as evenly as possible. Cover the furrow with the soil that was pushed to the side and pat down gently to press the seeds into the soil.

> **Tip:** When using the broadcasting method, a helpful strategy is to mix the seeds with sand, so that each child can scatter a big handful containing just a few seeds.

Broadcasting works well for tiny seeds, like lettuce, that are hard to distribute one by one. Show students how to gently sprinkle a handful of seeds — like confetti! — across the soil surface, distributing them as evenly as possible. This may sound simple, but it can be tricky for small hands and you'll probably have some thinning to do later on. Once the seeds are scattered, have students sprinkle more soil mix on top to just cover them. Finally, have the children press down gently on the soil with their hands.

After planting the seeds, it's time to water. Water newly planted seeds with care; it is easy to wash them out of the soil with a stream of water. Using a watering can with a sprinkler attachment, make a pass across your containers, pausing to allow water to soak in before making another pass. You've watered enough when the soil feels evenly moist when you poke your finger down to the level of your seeds. For general Watering Tips, see p. 97.

Check your container garden regularly to monitor the plants' growth. To keep plants producing, harvest vegetables and flowers as soon as they mature. Use a liquid organic fertilizer, such as fish emulsion, or add finished compost or worm castings every other week when you water. Plant new seeds or seedlings when you remove spent plants.

TYING IT TOGETHER   Create labels for each type of seed sown, including the name of the plant and the days until germination. Ask children, *What will these seeds need to grow? How can we take care of them?* Students can feed their seeds with handfuls of compost, worm castings, water, and even nice words and songs. Continue to water and wait, counting the days together until you start to see some green poking through the soil. As the plants grow, have children describe, illustrate, and measure what they see every few days. (Children can measure with rulers, but can also measure using parts of their bodies, such as a knuckle, finger, fist, or arm-length).

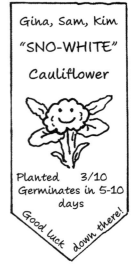

Gina, Sam, Kim
"SNO-WHITE"
Cauliflower

Planted   3/10
Germinates in 5-10 days
Good luck down there!

DIGGING DEEPER   After planting, take a picture of your children with their new garden. Take another picture every two weeks or so to track the progress of the garden.

One fun way to organize your garden is by planting theme beds or containers, such as a salsa or pizza bed, or a butterfly garden. See Theme Bed Ideas, p. 14, for suggestions.

Try planting "letters" or "numbers" by thickly sowing seeds in the desired shape. Watch the sprouts emerge and invite the children to touch the seedlings for a tactile experience with the letter or number.

RECOMMENDED AGES: 2+ ✿ INSIDE/OUTSIDE ✿ ANY SEASON

Root View Cups

DESCRIPTION   Children plant a variety of seeds in clear cups and observe the development of different root systems over time.

BACKGROUND   Different types of plants have different root systems. Some plants have a taproot — one main root growing downward with small hair-like roots coming off of it. A carrot is an example of a taproot we eat. Conversely, fibrous root systems branch repeatedly with no single main root. Grasses and lettuce are examples of plants with fibrous root systems. Legumes, such as beans and peas, have an additional root feature. Legumes turn nitrogen from the air into a form plants can use through special nodules on their roots. Exploring these nodules is a wonderful activity for young children because they can be seen without magnification.

Because all roots grow away from light, it's important to keep light-blocking paper sleeves on these root view cups when the children are not actively observing the roots.

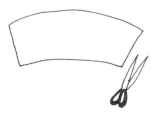    

MATERIALS
* ✿ Sharp tool or drill (for adult use)
* ✿ Clear plastic 8- to 10-oz cups
* ✿ Dark construction paper or card stock
* ✿ Scissors (for adult use)
* ✿ Seed-starting mix, homemade (combine 5 parts compost, 4 parts garden soil, 1 part sand) or commercial
* ✿ Hand trowels
* ✿ Seeds from a variety of plants with contrasting root types (for example, beets, wheat, and beans)
* ✿ Watering can
* ✿ Tape
* ✿ Markers

PREPARATION   Using a sharp tool or drill, punch three or four holes in the bottom of each cup for drainage.

Cut out a paper sleeve for each root view cup. To make a template for the sleeves, cut straight down one side of a cup, then cut off the bottom and the top rim. You should end up with an arch shape that you can lay flat and trace onto construction paper. Elongate one end of the arch to create a sleeve that can overlap at the seam and be taped.

ACTIVITY   Give each child or group of children a cup and show them how to carefully fill it with seed-starting mix. Help children plant three or four different seeds in each cup. To plant each seed, an adult should place a seed on the soil surface right against the side of the cup; as the adult holds the cup, a child can use the drill method (see p. 58) to push each seed into the soil. Plant the seed at a depth of roughly 2 times its width, or the depth indicated on the seed packet. Have the child gently press soil over the seed. When you're done, you should be able to see the seeds through the side of the clear cup.

Write the type of seed, child's name, date, etc. on a paper sleeve. Have children decorate the sleeves, perhaps with drawings predicting how the roots will look. Wrap the sleeve around the cup and tape it in place. Make sure the tape only touches the paper (not the plastic), so that the sleeve can slide easily on and off the cup. Explain that the sleeve is like a curtain to keep things nice and dark for the seed, but that the children can remove the sleeve whenever they want to see how the roots have grown. Water lightly to keep the soil moist, but not soggy, and place the cups — with sleeves on — in a warm, sunny spot.

Before the seeds sprout, find out what the children know about roots. Ask, *What do you think the roots will look like? Will roots be the same on different kinds of plants? Do all plants have roots? Why?* Record the children's ideas.

Meet with groups of children to monitor the roots' growth every two or three days. Compare the roots from the different kinds of seeds the children planted. Encourage the children to observe how each root grows out of its seed. *Do other roots branch off the main root? Which roots grow fastest? Which grow slowest? Do the roots grow faster or slower than the shoots? What direction are the roots growing? How about the shoots?*

TYING IT TOGETHER

Using your list of the children's original thoughts about roots, discuss the growth of the roots. Ask, *How did our roots grow? Do they look the same or different from what we thought? Do all roots grow in the same way? What do the roots do for the plant?*

DIGGING DEEPER

Bring in examples of different roots — weeds from the garden, radishes, carrots, etc. Have the children collect their own roots from the garden or a patch of weeds. Encourage them to sort the roots they find. They can sort by color, shape, size, etc.

Have the children draw pictures of the roots as they develop in their root-view cups or draw different kinds of roots.

Take a walk around the schoolyard or neighborhood to find places where roots have heaved up sidewalks or pavement.

Install a root view box in your garden so that children can observe larger root systems over longer periods of time. Root view boxes are also great for watching how water moves through soil and around root systems. (See Root View Boxes, p. 115.)

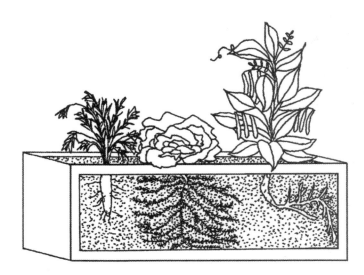

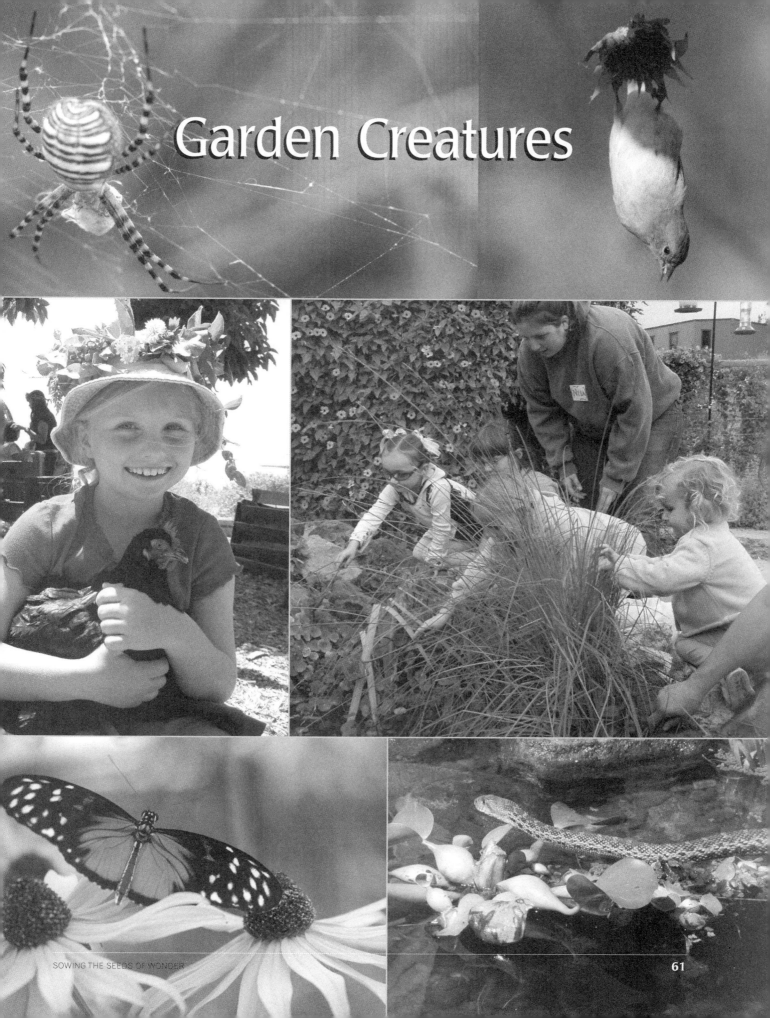

Garden Creatures

Child Development Center

HARTNELL COLLEGE, SALINAS, CA

Janice Martinez explains that the inspiration for the Hartnell College Child Development Center garden stemmed from a spring garden party, when the children, ages 3 to 5, planted sunflowers in a long narrow area along the back fence of the playground. In the fall, when they returned to school, the fence line was full of tall, bright yellow sunflowers. Together, Janice and the children explored the flowers and found a variety of insects on the plants. With the help of insect books, they discovered they had ladybug eggs, larva, pupa, and ladybugs living in the sunflowers, which were also full of aphids (ladybug food!). The children shared their new discoveries with their parents, siblings, and visitors. And the excitement kept building every time someone found something new. The children observed butterflies, bees, ants, spiders, and worms — all living in the small garden.

HARTNELL COLLEGE CHILD DEVELOPMENT CENTER

Several months later the children noticed that the sunflowers had developed seeds, which sparked a new area of interest. They harvested the seeds and saved them to plant in the spring. They also explored different types of seeds using pumpkins and corn. The center's curriculum, based on the children's interests, began to revolve around the garden and science.

The children's enthusiasm led the center to enlarge its garden the following year. A committee of teachers and parents designed and built a garden that incorporated the interests of the children, teachers, and parents. The children planted vegetables, sunflowers, and a butterfly garden. Everyone involved celebrated the new garden at the annual garden party. Features still to come include a rock garden, a tunnel, compost boxes, and a worm bin.

Favorite garden activities include planting seeds, watering, looking for bugs, harvesting, digging, and reading books. Many social interactions happen as the children work together or share something they've discovered. When a child finds something new, he or she calls everyone to come and see. Some children run to get magnifying glasses. If they discover an insect or worm, the children gently hold it. After observing the creature for a while, they release it in the garden — "to their home," as the children say. The garden has become a place that nurtures relationships and respect, confidence and collaboration. It is the life of the school!

Janice's love of gardening stems from growing up with gardening experiences on her grandparents' farm. "It just came naturally to share that passion with the children," she says. When she began gardening with children, she observed their daily joy and interest and quickly understood that the garden would serve as an outstanding classroom: in it the children would develop cognitive and language skills, problem-solving, large and small motor skills, and more. "The children also connect with the earth and environment, develop respect for living things, and learn where fruits and vegetables come from."

Gardening at the Child Development Center has become a family legacy. When one child's mom came to help plant sunflower seeds, her two-year-old son, Nicholas, tagged along and planted his own sunflower seed in a peat pot. Two weeks later, at the spring garden party, Nicholas planted his sunflower seedling next to his sister's. "On his first day of school that fall," Janice remembers, "Nicholas ran out to the garden to find his sunflower. It made me appreciate how many connections and memories have been made in this garden!"

Critter Crawl

DESCRIPTION

Children meet some garden inhabitants by going on a hunt for critters. They then develop garden rules for the treatment of animals. This activity is best done with a group of six or fewer children.

BACKGROUND

Gardens provide homes and food for many small creatures. Some of these creatures make pests of themselves by munching on growing plants. Others help by cultivating the soil, eating garden pests, pollinating flowers, and cleaning up decaying matter. This activity is a good basis for many concepts, such as wildlife in the garden, respect for other animals, and the fostering of a healthy garden ecosystem. This is also an important activity for brainstorming rules about respecting animals in your garden.

MATERIALS

For each pair of children:
❀ Small plastic cups or empty food containers
❀ *Jack's Garden* by Henry Cole
❀ *(Optional) Hey Little Ant!* by Phillip and Hannah Hoose
❀ 1 collection jar (use a plastic food container with holes punched in the lid)
❀ 1 hand lens or bug box
❀ 1 large white bed sheet
❀ Field guides, books, or literature on insects and small creatures

PREPARATION

If you can, prepare traps for insects and other small creatures the night before you do this activity. Sink a number of plastic cups or food containers into the soil in various places around your garden. Make sure the rims of the containers are even with the soil surface. Crawling insects will drop into the containers, allowing you to observe them in the morning. Do not set out traps if rain is expected, as the insects may drown in water that collects in the cup.

ACTIVITY

Sit in a circle with the children and read *Jack's Garden* to get them thinking about creatures in the garden. Ask, *Who lives in our garden? Who visits the garden?* Record their ideas. Tell the children they will be going on a hunt for small creatures in the garden. Explain that many critters live in the garden — some are helpful to the plants and some might hurt the plants — but the garden is their home. As a group, decide on some rules for how to treat any creatures you find. These might include: "Don't step on bugs," "Don't pick up anything if you don't know what it is or if you think it might be harmful," or "Treat other creatures as you would like to be treated." Reading *Hey Little Ant* can help to make this

point.

Ask, *Where do you think we might find creatures in the garden?* Record the children's ideas. If relevant, explain that you have also set out some traps for creatures that live in the soil and that you will inspect the traps together.

Take a small group of children out to the garden armed with a collecting container and bug boxes or hand lenses. If you set out traps, check them with the children. Look at seedlings and maturing plants in the garden. Watch for animals in action as they eat, pollinate, or crawl on the plants. Encourage the children to look for clues. Ask, *Can anyone see any holes, slime trails, or other trails left by animals?* Place the large white bed sheet under a plant and shake the plant. Any hidden critters should fall onto the sheet. Turn over leaves, rocks, and debris. When you find a small animal, carefully observe its behavior with the children before you collect it. Then gently encourage it to crawl into the jar using paper or a small stick. Catch flying insects by placing the jar quickly over the resting animal. Be careful to avoid any poisonous or stinging animals that may live in your area, including black widow and brown recluse spiders, scorpions, and centipedes. If you're unsure what poisonous creatures might reside in your area or what they look like, check with your cooperative extension office, or consult a field guide or the Internet before heading out to the garden.

Once you've trapped an animal, try to replicate its environment in the container. For instance, if you found it crawling on a branch, put a small branch in the container. If it is a soil dweller, add some soil to the container.

Each time you collect a creature, gather the children so that everyone can see it. Ask the children to observe it carefully and notice how it moves. *Does it have wings for flying? Does it creep, slide, glide or crawl? Can you find its mouth?*

When the group is finished observing the creatures, return any beneficial creatures to where you found them, and release any pests away from the garden.

TYING IT TOGETHER

Ask, *How many different types of creatures did we find in the garden? How are they alike? How are they different? How many animals can you find on one garden plant? Is the plant healthy?* Use a field guide to learn about the creatures you found. Are they friends or foes? If friends, ask, *What could we do to attract more of its kind to our garden?* If foes, think about how to deter them in the garden. To start, think about where you found each animal. Many garden pests hide under debris or in crevices beneath objects left lying around the garden. Perhaps you could clean up the garden, removing weeds, debris, and other likely hiding places for pests. Find out which predators eat the pest, and talk about ways you might lure these predators to your garden. For example, you might create a perennial border to make permanent homes for predator insects (see Tips for Creating a Healthy Garden Ecosystem, p. 110).

DIGGING DEEPER

Take a neighborhood walk with the children and count how many types of animals you can spot. Encourage the children to move like the animals they see!

Repeat the activity, this time observing the creatures in their own habitats rather than trapping them. Discuss how their behaviors are similar or different. Ask, *Do you think these bugs have families? Mommies? Daddies? Where do you think they go to eat? To sleep? To play?*

RECOMMENDED AGES: 2+ ✿ INSIDE/OUTSIDE ✿ ANY SEASON

Worm Study

DESCRIPTION

Children investigate worms using magnifying lenses, soil, leaves, and moist paper towels in an exploration station. This activity allows children to learn more about worms' behaviors and preferences.

BACKGROUND

Young children adore their cats, dogs, and other mammalian pets, but few will have observed other creatures very closely, especially invertebrates — animals without backbones — like worms. A worm lives in its own, underground world. It breathes through its skin and relies on the soil's moisture. A worm has no eyes, but can distinguish between light and dark. It has a varied diet of leaves, flowers, insects, and other decaying organisms, which it breaks down into nutrient-rich castings. It has no teeth, but eats its way through even hard-packed earth, loosening, aerating, and transforming it into fertile soil. It is deaf, but so sensitive to vibrations that wood turtles regularly stomp on the ground to call up worm dinners.

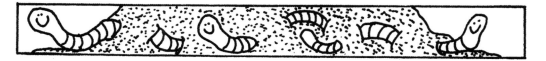

MATERIALS

* ✿ 4–6 spoons or trowels
* ✿ Worms
* ✿ 1 clear 1-liter plastic soda bottle
* ✿ Garden soil
* ✿ 1 old, dark-colored sock
* ✿ 4 empty tubs
* ✿ Several handfuls of freshly picked grass and tree leaves
* ✿ Water
* ✿ 1 moist paper towel per child
* ✿ 1 oilcloth or plastic tablecloth
* ✿ 4–6 hand or magnifying lenses
* ✿ 1 cup of uncooked oatmeal

PREPARATION

If you have a worm bin, you should have plenty of worms for this activity. If not, you'll need to find some. The day before you plan to collect the worms, moisten a patch of garden soil. Give each child a spoon or trowel, and take the group to the garden to unearth worms. Alternatively, you can buy earthworms at a bait shop.

Make a Worm Motel for your visitors by cutting off the top of a one-liter soda bottle. Fill the bottle about three-quarters full of soil. Add the worms. Pull an old, dark-colored sock up over the bottle to help keep out light.

Pour 1/2 inch or so of soil in the bottom of 2 tubs. Put about 1/4 inch of water in the third tub, and place the grass and leaves in the fourth. Moisten the paper towels. Finally, cover a table with the oilcloth or plastic tablecloth, or set up the station at an outside table. Put the Worm Motel, tubs, moist paper towels, and magnifying lenses on the table.

ACTIVITY Introduce the station by showing the children the Worm Motel, where their guest worms are staying. Share ideas about how to handle worms gently to avoid hurting them. With moist soil in your hand to protect the worm, show students how to gently pick a worm out of the Worm Motel and put it onto a moist paper towel for observation. Let the children know that worms are harmless and do not bite.

Ask volunteers to review the use of hand lenses or magnifying glasses. Tell the children they can hold the worms, put them on a moist paper towel to look at, and observe how the worms act when they put some soil, water, grass, or leaves on the towel with the worm. Help each child take out a worm and place it on his or her towel for observation. Tell children to return the worms to the Worm Motel after observing them.

At the end of the day or period, place a few spoonfuls of oatmeal in the Worm Motel for food. Cover the soil with moist leaves. (Do not use oily or aromatic leaves such as eucalyptus or bay laurel.) Pull the sock up over the motel, and place it in a cool spot out of direct sunlight.

TYING IT TOGETHER After all the children have had a chance to explore the worm station, be sure to put the worms back where they were found. If you purchased worms, you can release them into any open soil patch. If you have a worm bin, return the worms to it. Ask the children to imagine what the worms will do once they are released. Then ask, *What did you notice about worm behavior? What do you think worms do in the garden? What would it be like to be a worm in the garden?*

DIGGING DEEPER As children prepare a garden bed, have them collect and count all the worms they find. When returning the worms to the garden, help children distribute them evenly.

What do worms like to eat? Have children put different kinds of food, such as a piece of leaf, a flake of oatmeal, or a scrap of food in the Worm Motel. Ask children to check once a day to see what happens to the food.

Before releasing worms from the Worm Motel in the garden, have children count them to see if there are more or fewer guests than were put in the Motel. Have a creature release party so the children can celebrate the time they spent with the worms.

RECOMMENDED AGES: 2⁺ ✻ INSIDE/OUTSIDE ✻ ANY SEASON

Animal Charades

DESCRIPTION Children observe and mime garden animal behavior. This activity gives children an opportunity to look through the eyes of common garden animals and, in this way, develop empathy for these creatures. It also provides a strong foundation for further exploration of many concepts, including wildlife in the garden, respect for other animals, and garden ecology.

BACKGROUND Each animal in the garden develops unique characteristics depending on its lifestyle. Animals that live in the soil move, hear, and see differently from those that live on sticks or leaves. Children can observe these behaviors and compare them in a number of ways. Taking the time to encourage careful observation techniques will enhance the children's learning while ensuring the safety of the animals.

MATERIALS ✻ One container (such as a cottage cheese tub) with air holes in the lid

   For each group of 6–8 children:
   ✻ 10–12 individuals of the animal to be investigated (worms, sow bugs, ladybugs, snails, crickets, spiders, etc.)
   ✻ 3–4 clear plastic cups
   ✻ 1 white or light-colored sheet
   ✻ 1 small, plastic animal
   ✻ 5–10 leaves
   ✻ 5–10 plant stems about 6 inches long
   ✻ Dish of water
   ✻ Lamp or flashlight

PREPARATION On the day you plan to conduct the activity, collect the desired number of individuals of one type of garden animal and place them in the container. When ready, place two animals in each of the plastic cups. Conduct this activity in teacher-directed groups of 4–6 children.

ACTIVITY Gather your students in a circle around the sheet. Before releasing any animals, review ways to show respect to animals. If you and your students brainstormed rules in Critter Crawl, you can review them now.
   Place a plastic animal in the center of the circle, and have students practice observing with their eyes and not their hands. With their hands in their laps, children are able to focus

on the animal rather than what they can do to the animal. By sharing their observations in the small group, they are able to stay focused longer. Make a game of this by encouraging each child to offer a new observation about the animal, and see how many times you can go around the circle.

Once the children appear ready to observe a living animal in this same way, show them an animal that you collected and ask for their ideas about its behavior. *What do you know about this animal? What kinds of things does it do? How do you know? How could we learn more about what it does?* Tell children that after they watch how the animals behave, they will act out what the animals do.

The children may want to set up a prop, such as leaves, plant stems, or a dish of water, in front of the animal to see how it responds. Discuss what it might do when it sees water, food, or light, then test your theories by adding one of those elements to the circle and observing the animal's response. (If you add a dish of water, don't place the animals in the dish; just place it in the circle and watch to see if the animals approach it.)

Demonstrate how to gently tickle an animal to encourage movement. Each observation will give children more information. As they continue, stimulate the children to develop their own questions about the animal. Give them opportunities to design their own simple (and safe) ways to investigate their questions.

Now put the animals back in their containers. Ask the children to take turns acting out the animal's behavior in the center of the circle. Challenge them to act out a variety of behaviors and allow others to guess which animal they are mimicking. After everyone has had a chance to perform, see if anyone can watch the animal and discover a new behavior.

Finally, thank the animals for their time, and return them to the places where they were originally found.

TYING IT TOGETHER

As children watch the animals in each of the scenarios described above, encourage them to share observations with the group. *What is this animal doing that you could do?* Ask each child to select one behavior they want to mimic. Challenge the children to compare the behavior of the animals and themselves. *Do garden animals act like people? How? Do they act differently from people? How?*

DIGGING DEEPER

Let children experiment with a lamp or flashlights to discover how their animal behaves around bright light. Be sure to provide a dark place for the animals to take refuge.

Make a simple maze and let children experiment to see if the animal can be enticed through the maze in search of food, water, or a dark place to hide.

RECOMMENDED AGES: 4+ ❋ INSIDE/OUTSIDE ❋ ANY SEASON

Bird Feeders

DESCRIPTION

Children make a simple bird feeder from recycled materials. This activity, combined with Bird Observation, prompts children to explore the wonder of these very important and classic garden creatures.

BACKGROUND

Watching birds in the garden can occupy hours for the curious preschooler. Children can encourage birds to hang around their garden by building a simple feeder. Birds are important visitors as they eat many would-be plant pests. House wrens can collect thousands of insects a day to feed their young. Birds also grace the garden with beautiful music as they communicate with each other. Birds need to eat a tremendous amount of food to sustain their busy lifestyles, and many of the same birds who feast on insects will also eat birdseed, crumbs, and other treats from a feeder.

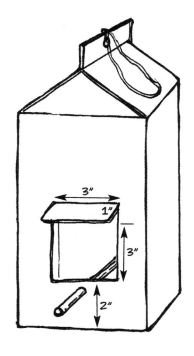

Some birds stay in an area all year long, while other birds migrate with the seasons. A bird feeder can provide a snack for birds on the wing and may bring in some occasional visitors. As children's interest grows, you may want to check out a bird field guide from your local library to help with identification.

MATERIALS

❋ Sharp scissors or an X-acto knife (for adult use)
❋ Hole punch

For each child:
❋ One cardboard milk carton (at least one-quart size)
❋ 12" long stick or dowel
❋ Duct tape
❋ String
❋ Birdseed
❋ Glue, construction paper scraps, yarn, paint, etc.
❋ (Optional) Contact paper

PREPARATION

Thoroughly wash out the milk cartons. For each carton, cut a 3"x 3" door opening in one wall of the carton about 2" above the base of the carton. Extend the side cuts another inch toward the top of the carton and fold the resulting flap at the top of the opening so that it makes a small protective eave for a visiting bird.

Punch a hole through the front and back of each carton just below the opening, and poke a stick or dowel through the holes to make a perch. Secure the stick with duct tape on the inside if necessary. Punch a hole in the top of the carton and pull a string through. Tie the string to make a loop for hanging.

ACTIVITY

Gather the children around a table and tell them they will be designing feeding stations for birds. These will not be houses for birds, just places for them to get a snack. Discuss why birds need so much food and how providing food might bring more birds to the garden. Remind the children that, while some birds eat plants and could harm the garden, many birds also eat pests, and thus help the garden.

Where in the garden do you often see birds? What colors do they seem to like? What objects? What decorations do you think might attract the birds? Let the children be creative with decorating the milk cartons, using paint, construction paper, yarn, etc. Remind them that the milk carton feeders will get wet in the rain, so the decorations might change as time goes by. You may choose to cover each feeder with contact paper to help it last longer.

When the feeders are finished, take them out to the garden and decide where to put them. Try to spread them out so that birds can visit different parts of the garden. The sites should be out of the wind and preferably near the protective shelter of trees or bushes. If you've decided to build a bird blind (next activity) be sure to place the feeders within observation distance of it. You may also choose to locate your bird feeders within view of a classroom window to allow for observation from indoors. Fill the feeders with birdseed. Ask the children how long they think it will be before the birds find the feeders.

TYING IT TOGETHER

Watch the feeders every day with the children. Ask, *Do you notice more birds in the garden? How many different types of birds can you spot?* Replenish the bird feeders as needed.

DIGGING DEEPER

For food, you can also try peanuts, crumbs, sunflower seeds, or popcorn. Watch to see what the birds prefer.

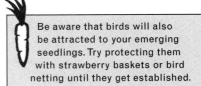

Be aware that birds will also be attracted to your emerging seedlings. Try protecting them with strawberry baskets or bird netting until they get established.

Make natural bird feeders. Let flowers such as sunflowers go to seed on the plant or smear a pinecone with peanut butter and roll it in birdseed.

Many plants attract birds to the garden. They love to eat berries from plants such as pyracanthus, blackberry, hawthorn, and viburnum. Hummingbird-friendly flowers include trumpet vine, hummingbird and pineapple sage, nasturtium, and penstemon. Work with older students or volunteers to design a special area of the garden for birds.

Provide a bathing and drinking spot for bird friends with a hanging birdbath that's out of reach of children.

RECOMMENDED AGES: 4+ ❋ INSIDE/OUTSIDE ❋ ANY SEASON

Bird Observation

DESCRIPTION A bird blind is a semi-permanent garden element through which children can observe and study birds.

BACKGROUND Birds are highly sensitive to nearby disturbances. Young children might have a hard time getting close enough to birds to observe them without scaring them away. A bird blind is easy to construct and may help children sneak up closer to see birds in a way they never have before. Plus, children love to "outsmart" the birds with their camouflage!

MATERIALS
* ❋ Sharp scissors (for adult use)
* ❋ 1 or 2 old sheets
* ❋ 2 6' stakes, plus 2 short stakes (if needed)
* ❋ 50' of rope
* ❋ 2 lb birdseed
* ❋ (Optional) Binoculars

PREPARATION Make a bird blind by cutting eyes holes in a sheet at an appropriate height for your students.

Find an area in the garden to hang the bird blind. This should be a place with little disturbance and high bird activity, perhaps near the bird feeders the class made in the previous activity. If this spot is near a chain-link fence, poke multiple holes along the top and down the sides of the sheet. Feed rope through each hole and tie it around the fence links.

If there's no chain-link fence nearby, pound two 6' stakes into the ground and tie the sheet to them. To stabilize the stakes, pound two smaller stakes into the ground about two feet from the tall ones. Tie the rope around each tall stake and stretch it tight to the smaller stakes. Make multiple holes across the top and bottom of the sheet. Feed rope through holes across the top and bottom and fasten the rope to the tops and bottoms of the tall stakes. Your bird blind is done!

The day or morning before your students visit the bird blind, toss some handfuls of birdseed on the ground in front of it to attract birds.

ACTIVITY Introduce the students to the bird blind by asking how close they think they can get to birds without scaring them away. Explain that birds are always flying here and there, so you never know when some might be right on the other side of our bird blind. Before approaching, ask the children, *What do you think scares birds? Why? How might we get closer without scaring them?* Share ideas about how to approach the blind appropriately. Slowly and quietly walk them to the blind. Bringing smaller groups to bird blind with an adult or older student might help with the management of this activity.

If no birds are present, talk with children about how we might attract birds to the area. Have children suggest times that we might come back, foods we could put on the other side, or new locations for the blind.

If there are birds on the other side of the blind, have the students quietly describe characteristics of the birds, such as colors, sizes, and shapes. Encourage students to focus on the birds' beaks, feathers, and feet. Ask, *Why are these things useful to birds?*

Discuss how birds react when they see or hear other animals nearby. Ask the children if and how the birds tell each other that there are intruders nearby.

For children working on learning numbers, have them count all the birds they see. If this goes well, challenge them to count how many wings and feet they see.

After leaving the bird blind, use the students' basic descriptions to see if you can identify the birds from a local bird field guide.

As in the Animal Charades activity, have the children act out the different things they see the birds doing. Mimic the way the bird flies, glides, and swoops. Can they imitate how birds talk to one another? Ask, *Do all birds fly in straight lines? Do all birds flap their wings? How do birds move on the ground?*

TYING IT TOGETHER

Have children draw the birds they saw. You may need to help them remember the colors and other features they noticed. Then make a storybook about the birds in your garden. Ask the children to invent stories about what it's like to fly, live in a nest, or eat worms. Use the pictures they drew to illustrate the book.

DIGGING DEEPER

Use the children's observations and the knowledge they gained about different birds to create a birding field guide for your bird blind.

Sprinkle birdseed right outside the classroom and watch the birds that visit through a window. Have children compare and contrast these birds to the ones that visit the garden. Ask, *What do you think that bird is saying? Does it sound calm? Happy? Nervous? Hungry? To whom do you think the bird is calling?* Have your students name the birds based on characteristics they notice, such as "fluffy blue hairdo bird."

Look for old birds nests. Dissect them with the children and discuss what birds use to build their nests and why.

Harvest, Cooking, and Art Activities

Rooftop Greenhouse Garden

ST. HILDA'S & ST. HUGH'S SCHOOL, NEW YORK, NY

St. Hilda's & St. Hugh's is an independent Episcopal school for students in grades PreK–8. Children of all ages use the rooftop greenhouse and engage in related classroom activities. Karen Doeblin is a part-time greenhouse keeper, who works with faculty to plan programs. She explains that learning in the greenhouse is perfect for preschoolers because it involves everything from the tactile to the mysterious. "We stress that plants need tending and the children must be the caretakers. Typically, they are careful and nurturing — I am always impressed by how responsible they are when it comes to the plants!" she says, and adds that gardening helps children practice many fine and gross motor skills. They dig in containers and use two hands to water. They shell peas to see where seeds come from, munching the peas as they shell! They are always enthusiastic participants. Karen loves to hear children ask, "Is this enough dirt?" "Is my seed deep enough?" "Did I give it enough water?" Or, this tentative question when they pick something: "Can I *really* eat it?"

For children in New York City or other urban areas, playing in dirt, growing plants, and harvesting them can be unique experiences. A greenhouse or garden provides a vital connection to environmental processes, including the cycles of nature. These experiences also build a sense of competence, as children harvest something of value from the soil, like a carrot, or overcome a fear of dirty hands, worms, or bugs.

ST. HILDA'S & ST. HUGH'S

Karen offers these tips to anyone planning to garden with young children:

❀ Review rules and how-to's often. These might include: how to respect the area and tools, how to ask before eating anything, how to use a watering can or trowel, or how to treat a worm or ladybug. Assume nothing!

❀ Use a garden layout that offers nooks and crannies to explore, yet keeps the children visible. For instance, put plants at multiple heights so students can look up and down. Also use multiple work stations, short worktables, and a variety of containers for planting in and for "free digging." Provide enough plastic trowels, watering cans, and aprons for each student to use their own, and have a place where students can make a mess that you can easily hose down.

❀ Remember that a garden environment is different from the classroom. To help children adjust to the space, encourage them to observe and explore before diving into a structured activity.

❀ Have a plan for each session, but keep it simple and leave lots of time for free digging and watering. Children love to water!

❀ Do lots of planting, even though some seeds won't sprout. Kids love to put seeds in soil. Because only some plants survive, consider *not* labeling plants with children's names.

❀ Grow plants that germinate quickly, such as lettuce or grass, or have seeds that are easy for small hands to manage. Children can broadcast small lettuce or grass seeds (see p. 58) and see results in a few days. Beans are big and easy to hold on to; children love to poke these seeds into the soil. Plants with small seeds that germinate slowly (e.g. carrots) are best planted by adults for everyone to enjoy harvesting later.

❀ Connect the garden to the children's lives — Ask, *Why do we plant seeds in a small pot? Why do babies start in a crib, then move to a bigger bed?* — and to what they are reading. In spring Karen's ECE classes read *Peter Rabbit* or *Benjamin Bunny* and then plant something featured in the story. They read *Tops and Bottoms* to teach the children about plant structures and edible parts of plants.

RECOMMENDED AGES: 2+ ❋ OUTSIDE ❋ SPRING, SUMMER, FALL

Solar Tea

DESCRIPTION

On a hot, sunny day, children gather fresh herbs they've grown in the garden and capture the sun's energy to make delicious sun tea.

BACKGROUND

Just like regular tea, Solar Tea uses heat to diffuse the flavor of the herbs in water. The longer the tea brews and the more leaves you use, the stronger the flavor and the darker the color of the tea will be. You can use a variety of fresh or dried plants for tea, including peppermint, spearmint, chamomile flowers, lemongrass, and lemon verbena.

CAUTION: Strictly supervise children harvesting herbs to be sure they don't accidentally harvest the wrong plant. Some garden plants and weeds are toxic, so always make sure you know what's going into the tea. If you're unsure whether a plant is safe to use, consult your local cooperative extension office or another reliable source.

MATERIALS

* ❋ Handfuls of leaves from suitable plants (see examples above)
* ❋ Scissors
* ❋ Large, clean glass jars with lids
* ❋ Water
* ❋ Strainer
* ❋ Cups
* ❋ (Optional) Ice cubes
* ❋ (Optional) Honey or sugar

ACTIVITY

Gather the children in the garden. Tell them they're going to make tea today with herbs from the garden and help from the sun! Together, walk to the first plant for harvest. Invite the children to pick a leaf, rub it between their fingers, and smell it. Ask, *Would this taste good in our tea?* If so, help children collect a few sprigs of the desired plant. Have a child grasp a twig he or she wants to harvest, while you snip it off at the base with scissors. Repeat the process with any other plants you'll be using. Wash the sprigs carefully and pat them dry. Place the clean sprigs on a table the children can work on.

Have the children wash their hands thoroughly. Ask the children to pull the leaves off the stems, trying to keep the leaves from each type of plant separate. Let them know it's okay if the leaves get torn; it makes the tea stronger. Ask, *Are there any leaves you think might taste good together in a tea? Shall we make a tea that has a mix of herbs, or a separate tea for each herb?* Try making several jars of tea with different combinations or with single herbs. Fill the jars with water and immerse the fresh leaves.

Screw lids on the jars and set the jars in a sunny

spot. Let children place their hands on the jar to feel how warm or cool the water is. Ask, *Does the water feel warm or cool to you now? How warm do you think it will get in the sun?* Let the tea sit for 2 to 3 hours and feel for warmth again. *How does it feel now?* Shake the jar to mix the contents thoroughly. Add honey or sugar and ice if you wish. Pour through a strainer into cups, serve, and enjoy!

TYING IT TOGETHER

Encourage the children to taste each variety of tea they created and describe the different flavors.

When everyone has tasted all the Solar Teas, have the class vote on their favorite. Help them create a larger batch of this flavor for a special day or parent visit.

DIGGING DEEPER

Plant a "tea bed" in your garden so you will always have the right plants for tea all in one place.

Homemade dried tea blends are a fun craft and make wonderful gifts. Harvest plentiful quantities of the plants and dry them by hanging small bunches of each type in a warm, dark place. When they are very dry, have the children tear off the leaves and mix the different varieties together. Package these in airtight containers with labels colored by the children.

RECOMMENDED AGES: 2+ ❋ INSIDE/OUTSIDE ❋ SUMMER, FALL, WINTER

Winter Squash Tasting

DESCRIPTION Children taste several kinds of winter squash and describe each squash's color, shape, taste, and texture.

BACKGROUND Winter squash is grown in the summer, but gets its name from the fact that it stores well and is therefore a good vegetable for winter eating. Young children often enjoy the sweet flavor and soft texture of baked winter squash. These vegetables are also high in fiber and vitamin A, making them a good food for children to include in a healthy diet.

MATERIALS
- ❋ 2 each of several types of winter squash, such as butternut, acorn, delicata, red kuri, pie pumpkin, or blue hubbard
- ❋ Large sharp knife, large spoon, fork (for adult use)
- ❋ Olive oil
- ❋ Baking pans or cookie sheets
- ❋ Spatula
- ❋ (*Optional*) Heavy cream, salt, empty glass jar with lid, butter knife — for making butter
- ❋ (*Optional*) Salt — for roasting seeds
- ❋ Napkins

PREPARATION Reserve one squash of each type you'll be tasting to show children what it looked like originally. Using an oven, roast the second squash of each type. Preheat the oven to 350°F. Cut each squash in half, scoop out the seeds and stringy innards, and poke the skin a few times with a fork. Rub olive oil onto the cut edges and place the squash, cut edges down, in a baking pan. Bake until the squash is soft and easy to dent when pressed, about 45 minutes. Let the squash cool slightly, then scoop out enough pieces for each child to try a bite. Squash is tastiest when served warm; if roasting ahead of time, you can reheat the squash in an oven or microwave.

ACTIVITY Introduce each squash by showing the unroasted vegetable and asking for descriptions of its color and shape. Show what the same type looks like after roasting. As the children taste each kind of squash, ask them about the taste and texture and record their answers. You can also invite the children to taste the roasted seeds (roasting instructions below) and describe those flavors and textures. Have them vote on their favorite kinds of squash and seeds.

    Roasting squash seeds (optional). You can roast the seeds of each squash separately, and keep track of which seeds go with which squash, or simply roast all the seeds together. Separate the seeds from the stringy squash innards (kids with clean hands can help), place seeds on a cookie sheet, drizzle with a small amount of olive oil, and sprinkle with salt. Stir to coat all the seeds, and place in the oven at 350°F. Check the seeds every 10 minutes or so, stirring them each time, until the seeds are slightly browned and crispy. Cool the seeds and enjoy.

Making butter (optional). If you wish, have the children make butter to put on the warm squash. Fill an empty glass jar $1/4$ full with heavy whipping cream and a dash of salt. Screw the lid on tightly, and have the children wrap their hands around the jar and shake vigorously. The process is faster if you let the cream come to room temperature first, or if the children have warm hands. The cream first becomes whipped cream, then butter. You can tell it's butter when the cream has separated into a lump of solid butter and a puddle of buttermilk. Stop shaking at this point to avoid melting the butter. Drain off and discard the salty buttermilk. Spread the butter on pieces of squash as you hand them out to the children.

TYING IT TOGETHER

Encourage the children to think about this activity and all the taste-testing they've done. Ask, *What did you think the winter squash would taste like? What do you think of winter squash now? Which kind of squash did you like best? Did everyone like the same kinds best?*

DIGGING DEEPER

After the children have chosen their favorite kinds of squash, have them plant those varieties in your garden in the spring. If you saved seeds from last year's squash plants, they will grow into new squash plants, but they will not necessarily produce the same type of squash. Therefore, if you know you want to grow a specific type of particularly tasty squash, it is best to use packaged seeds. You can use the resulting vegetables for a variety of cooking activities the next school year, since most winter squashes work well in any recipes calling for pumpkin (and also make a great snack on their own).

Tip: If you grow winter squash, there are several storage techniques you can use to keep them as long as possible. First, leave the squashes on the vine until the stem has turned brown and the vines are drying up. If possible, cut each squash stem so it's three or four inches long. Never carry a squash by the stem (if the stem breaks off, the squash rots). Leave the squashes outside in the sun for a week to cure, then store them in a cool, dark place such as a shed or basement. Place the squashes so that they are not touching each other. Check them periodically; if a squash develops a soft spot, you can cut that spot out and use the rest of the squash.

Hold a tasting with another fruit or vegetable. Try an apple tasting, with several varieties of apples from a farmers market; a tomato tasting with samples from the garden, a farmers market, and a supermarket; or a roasted root vegetable tasting, with carrots, beets, rutabagas, parsnips, taro, radishes, or other root crops.

RECOMMENDED AGES: 2+ ❋ INSIDE / OUTSIDE ❋ ANY SEASON

Garden Omelets

DESCRIPTION

Omelets provide a tasty and versatile way to use almost any herbs and vegetables growing in your garden.

BACKGROUND

Omelets are a great garden cooking activity because they provide a tasty, easy way to introduce children to new vegetables and herbs. In addition, small children enjoy participating in the food preparation by harvesting herbs and greens and tearing them into pieces with their fingers. Favorite omelet ingredients include basil, sage, oregano, spinach, chard, kale, onion tops, and garlic tops.

This activity is geared toward groups of six children, using one egg per person for a large group omelet. If there are more than six children in the group, it's best to make more than one omelet — an omelet larger than six eggs takes longer to cook through and is difficult to flip.

MATERIALS

* ❋ A variety of fresh herbs and vegetables from your garden or a market
* ❋ Scissors (for adult use)
* ❋ Large bowl
* ❋ Eggbeater
* ❋ Eggs (one per child)
* ❋ Knife to chop vegetables (for adult use)
* ❋ Cutting board
* ❋ Salt and pepper
* ❋ Stove or hotplate (for adult use)
* ❋ Large frying pan (for adult use)
* ❋ Butter
* ❋ 2 spatulas
* ❋ Grated cheese
* ❋ Plates — one for the hot omelet plus one per child
* ❋ Forks

PREPARATION

Tour your garden beforehand to assess which herbs and vegetables are available for harvest. If none are available, purchase a selection from the store or a farmer's market and plan to plant some seedlings with the children for future omelet making.

ACTIVITY

Make sure the children know what an omelet is when you introduce the activity. Ask, *Do you think we could find some ingredients for an omelet in our garden? Let's go take a look!* Walk through the garden with the children, pausing to consider ingredients both serious and silly. Ask, *How about a persimmon in our omelet? No? Okay, how about some of this basil?* Let the children take turns harvesting. Help children harvest herbs by instructing a child to hold a sprig while you cut it at the base with scissors. Have the children carry their harvested herbs and vegetables to the sink. Ask everyone to wash their hands, and wash the herbs and vegetables, as well.

At a table, ask the children to pull the herb leaves off the stems and tear up the leaves. While this is happening, have each child — one by one — go to an adult who has a large bowl and eggbeater. Let the child crack and beat one egg with the help of the adult. If your group harvested any vegetables that need chopping, have an adult helper prepare those vegetables. When the eggs are beaten, ask the children to add the herbs and vegetables to the bowl of eggs. Have a couple of children help you add some salt and pepper (have them shake the salt and pepper into their hands before putting it into the bowl, so you can control how much is added). Stir.

Heat the frying pan over medium-low heat and coat with butter. Pour the egg mixture into the pan. After a couple minutes, start checking periodically for doneness by sliding a spatula under the omelet. When the egg mixture is cooked most of the way through, flip the entire omelet over, using two spatulas (with an omelet this big, it's helpful to flip it to make sure it cooks all the way through). If it falls apart, you can call it a scramble and enjoy the feast anyhow! Next place the shredded cheese on one half of the omelet as it continues to cook and, once the underside is cooked, fold the omelet in half over the cheese (since this omelet is thick, the folded edge may break, which is fine). Turn off the heat, transfer the omelet to a plate, and let it cool slightly. Cut wedge-shaped slices for all the children and adult helpers, and serve. Have everyone wash their hands again. The children can eat their omelets warm with forks or, when cool enough, simply by holding the slices in their hands.

TYING IT TOGETHER

Review the origins of everything the children put into the omelet. Ask, *Where did the eggs come from? What about the herbs and vegetables? Does anyone know where the cheese came from?* (Our whole omelet came from plants and animals!) *Could you taste the garden in our omelet?* Have students share how the omelet tasted.

DIGGING DEEPER

You can also make garden-fresh pizza, salsa, salads, and snacks by having each child contribute one part.

Use a favorite garden-fresh treat to plan a theme bed with all of the ingredients for that particular recipe. For example, you could plant an omelet bed with vegetables and herbs for the omelet. For more Theme Bed ideas, see p. 14.

RECOMMENDED AGES: 3+ ❋ INSIDE/OUTSIDE ❋ ANY SEASON

Six-Seed Trail Mix

DESCRIPTION

Children make a nutritious snack from a variety of edible seeds. This is a fun activity to do after Seed Secrets (p. 49).

BACKGROUND

When we eat a meal or snack, we often forget that we are consuming parts of plants. For example: a carrot is a root, asparagus is a stem, lettuce is a leaf, broccoli is a collection of flower buds, a tomato is a fruit, and a pea is a seed! Most children don't know where many foods come from unless they have spent time in a garden or on a farm and observed food plants growing up close. In addition to gardening, we recommend using literature, movies, and Web sites to show children how food grows in the field or orchard.

> **SAFETY TIP:** Make sure you are aware of any food allergies in your classroom, particularly peanut allergies, a common one for young children. Adapt the activity appropriately for allergic children.

In this activity, children learn about six different foods that are seeds or contain seeds. This snack offers children a healthy energy boost because seeds are a good source of protein, giving us energy to work and play. This trail mix is especially nutritious because no extra fat, sugar, or salt has been added to the seeds.

Note: You might want to ask parents to help out by providing some of the ingredients for this activity.

MATERIALS

- ❋ A few peanuts in the shell
- ❋ Raw, unsalted, shelled peanuts
- ❋ A few walnuts in the shell
- ❋ Shelled walnuts
- ❋ A few almonds in the shell
- ❋ Shelled almonds
- ❋ A few pumpkin seeds in the shell
- ❋ Shelled pumpkin seeds
- ❋ A few sunflower seeds in the shell
- ❋ Shelled sunflower seeds
- ❋ A few grapes
- ❋ Raisins
- ❋ 6 large bowls or clean plastic containers
- ❋ 1 small drinking cup per student
- ❋ A plastic knife
- ❋ Photos of some of these seeds growing on a plant

PREPARATION

Pour the shelled seeds into the bowls or containers. Arrange them on a clean table and set out the paper cups. Have all children wash their hands carefully before beginning the activity.

ACTIVITY

Show the children the different nuts and seeds in and out of the shell. Ask, *Is a nut a seed? You bet! The walnut is the seed of the walnut tree. The almond is the seed of the almond tree. What do you think would happen if we planted and cared for a walnut or an almond?* Find out if anyone has seen a walnut growing on a tree, or if anyone knows how a peanut grows. Listen to the children's answers and show them actual examples or photos of the seeds growing on the plants. Explain that they will be making a healthy snack made up of six kinds of seeds and introduce each type of seed. When you get to the raisins, ask the children if they know where a raisin comes from. *Is it a seed? No, actually it is a fruit, but it still has seeds inside!* Show them a grape and cut it open to display the seeds. Explain that a raisin is just a dried grape. Pass out a raisin to each child and ask them to chew the raisins carefully. Ask, *Can you feel the tiny seeds inside?*

Invite children to visit the snack table in groups of 2 to 4. Ask them to count 5 items from each bowl into a paper cup. (Alternatively, you could let each child measure a spoonful of each item instead of counting.) When everyone has collected his or her six-seed trail mix, take the snack outside and eat it together in the garden. Be sure to thank the sun, soil, water, air, and plants for the food!

TYING IT TOGETHER

Ask, *How did your seed mix taste? Which seeds did you like best? What would happen if you planted those seeds?* You can also share with children that seeds give them a healthy energy boost because they contain all the energy needed for that baby plant to grow. *Can you feel the energy boost from your seedy snack? Let's go play a game and use some of the energy those seeds gave us!*

DIGGING DEEPER

Send home the recipe for six-seed trail mix and encourage families to make it for a school snack. Try some other variations of nuts and seeds in the mix.

After first asking parents about any food allergies, try another seed snack — for example, crackers (ground wheat seeds) with peanut butter (ground peanut seeds), or corn chips (ground corn seeds) with hummus (ground garbanzo bean seeds). Popcorn is a seed too!

Help students create seed mosaics. Simply paint a squiggly line or spiral of glue on a piece of paper, and allow students to sprinkle handfuls of mixed seeds over the top.

RECOMMENDED AGES: 4+ ✽ INSIDE/OUTSIDE ✽ ANY SEASON

My Edible Garden

DESCRIPTION

Children use their imaginations to create miniature "gardens" of vegetables and herbs on a cracker.

BACKGROUND

Children are far more likely to try new foods, and like them, if they have a hand in growing, harvesting, or preparing the foods. Children are especially likely to sample new foods if they are presented in a spirit of fun and adventure. This activity fosters creativity while encouraging children to try new vegetables and herbs.

MATERIALS

✽ A variety of herbs from the garden or a store, such as oregano, basil, rosemary, sage
✽ A variety of vegetables, such as broccoli, cucumber, carrot, lettuce, red bell pepper
✽ Edible flowers (if available) such as nasturtium, borage, calendula, or bachelor buttons
✽ Sharp knife to chop vegetables (for adult use)
✽ Cutting board
✽ Bowls
✽ Sunflower seeds
✽ Spoons
✽ Hummus, bean dip, or cream cheese
✽ Butter knife for spreading
✽ 1 large cracker per child
✽ (Optional) Paper towels

PREPARATION

If you are using any herbs, vegetables, and edible flowers from your garden, ask some or all of the children to help you harvest ahead of time. Wash and slice the herbs and vegetables into very small pieces (some vegetables, such as carrots or beets, work well when grated). Put them in bowls and arrange them on a table so that the children can sit at the table and reach all the bowls. Set out bowls of sunflower seeds. Place spoons in each bowl. Spread hummus, bean dip, or cream cheese on each cracker.

ACTIVITY

Take children on a walk to the garden and ask them to describe what they see there. Ask, *What are the parts of a garden?* (Plants, rocks, pathways, trees, soil, etc.) Tell the children they're going to use their imaginations to create their own miniature gardens today — and then they get to eat them!

Before gathering at the table, make sure everyone washes their hands. Show the children a cracker with spread. Tell them, *In my imaginary little garden, this will be the soil covering the ground.* Now demonstrate how to stick bits of vegetables and herbs into it to create a pretend garden. For example, a small broccoli floret might represent an apple tree. Shredded beets might become a brick pathway, etc. Show them all the vegetables, herbs, and seeds available to use and then give each child a cracker (on a paper towel, if desired). Sit the children at the table to build their edible gardens, and be prepared with extra crackers for children who drop theirs. As the children are creating their edible gardens, ask questions. Encourage them to describe their "garden" and what is growing in it.

Before eating the crackers, ask for volunteers to show and describe their edible gardens to the class.

Once everyone who wants to has shared his or her garden, it is time to feast! Since the eating will be messy, you may want to invite the children to eat their "gardens" outside over grass or even in their real garden!

TYING IT TOGETHER

Take a walk around the garden. Ask, *How is this garden like your pretend edible garden? How is it different? What would you like to add or change in our outdoor garden?*

DIGGING DEEPER

Teach the children about the six plant parts — roots, stems, leaves, flowers, fruits, and seeds. Collect a sample of each from the garden or a farmer's market and have the children create a cracker for each plant part!

Make edible rainbows using fruits and vegetables of every color on crackers spread with cream cheese.

RECOMMENDED AGES: 4+ ❋ INSIDE/OUTSIDE ❋ FALL, WINTER

Gourd Animals

DESCRIPTION   Children use their imaginations to design a "gourd animal" from a gourd they may have helped to plant, harvest, and cure.

BACKGROUND   People have grown gourds for centuries to use for bowls, bird feeders, instruments, art forms, and more. Gourds grow best in areas with hot summers. For this activity use one of three types of gourd: cucurbita, lagenaria, or luffa. Cucurbita gourds are highly cold-sensitive and ornamental, coming in various shapes and colors, some with bumps and other textures. Lagenaria gourds are hard-shelled and frost tolerant, maturing into late fall. Luffa gourds, which have a longer curing process than cucurbitas and lagenarias, look and feel somewhat like a sea sponge when cured. In fact, they are used to make luffa bath sponges. Consult a local gardener or your local extension office to determine the best type of gourd to grow in your area. Because your children will be turning these gourds into pets, consider varieties with shapes that resemble animals, like snake or swan gourds.

  As a fruit related to melons, gourds grow on vines that can climb trellises, fences, or a "gourd dome" (see p. 15 for more information). To keep the gourds off the ground, be sure to give the vine something sturdy to climb.

MATERIALS
❋ Gourds
❋ Newspaper
❋ Scissors (for adult use)
❋ Rubbing alcohol (for adult use)
❋ Decorating supplies, such as:
  – Nontoxic paints
  – Markers
  – Glue
  – Glitter
  – String, ribbon, or rope
  – Googley eyes

PREPARATION

Curing gourds takes some time, but the result is worth it! Your gourds are ready to pick when the once-green stems have turned brown. Use scissors to clip the gourds from the vine, leaving an inch or two of the stem attached to the gourd. Do this with care! Any bruise on the fruit increases its chances of rotting. Gently wash the gourds with warm, soapy water to remove dirt, and then wipe them down with rubbing alcohol to remove bacteria. Lay clean newspapers in a warm, dry, well-ventilated area and space the gourds on the newspaper so they aren't touching. Turn the gourds regularly and be sure to remove any that show signs of decay. After 4 to 6 weeks, the gourds should be fully dried. You'll know they're ready when the seeds rattle inside.

ACTIVITY

When your gourds are dried, create a work area for the children by laying down newspaper and setting out decorating supplies. Explain to the children that they're each going to get one gourd to decorate as an "animal." Show them how a long, narrow part might become a neck and a round part, a belly. Use paint to add wings, eyes, feet, and fur. Now, let the children decorate to their hearts' content!

TYING IT TOGETHER

This activity is a great way to expand a child's understanding of what can be done with fruit from their garden. They've explored soil, observed creatures, and eaten delicious food; now they get to create art! What else can they find in the garden that might be useful for making art?

DIGGING DEEPER

Have your students name their pets and create a story about them. Then, as a class, write one story that includes all the pets in the class as characters!

Take the biggest gourd from your harvest and make it the "class pet." The children can choose a name for it and collaborate on how to decorate it. Then, much like living class pets, each student can take it home for a weekend.

There are lots of other ways to use gourds, too. Their rattling seeds make many gourds amazing instruments! You can make sponges from luffa gourds and send them home as gifts for parents. Very young children may enjoy just feeling different gourds, playing music by rattling the seeds, or painting the surface of these hard-skinned fruits.

Appendix

For additional resources
not included in this book, visit
www.lifelab.org/pdfs/
EducationalGardenResources.pdf

Songs

Children love singing! We've included two of our favorite garden-themed songs below, and you can find words to many others on the Internet. We especially like the following songs from *www.preschooleducation.com*:

* **The Pumpkin Vine** (tune: Frere Jacques)
* **Planting Time** (tune: Row, Row, Row Your Boat)
* **Over In The Garden** (tune: Over in the Meadow)
* **The Seeds Grow** (tune: Farmer in the Dell)
* **Vegetables** (tune: Mary Had a Little Lamb)
* **Dig and Hoe** (tune: My Bonnie Lies Over the Ocean)

Flowers Growing Song
Tune: The Mulberry Bush; Copyright ©Jean Warren. Used with permission. Taken from *www.preschoolexpress.com*.

Have the children lay on the floor and curl up into balls. Have them pretend they are tiny seeds buried in the ground.

This is the way we sprout our roots,
Sprout our roots, sprout our roots.
This is the way we sprout our roots,
When spring time is here.

This is the way we pop through the dirt,
Pop through the dirt, pop through the dirt.
This is the way we pop through the dirt
When spring time is here.

Additional verses:
This is the way we stretch and grow.
This is the way we shoot up so tall.
This is the way we open our buds.
This is the way we bend in the breeze.
This is the way we smile at the sun.

Oh Little Apple
By Jim Marshall (free download at *www.jimmarshallmusic.com*)

One day I went to market,
On an afternoon in fall,
I saw the apple colors,
Red, yellow, green, and all.

Chorus:
Oh little apple, oh great big apple,
A red one, yellow one, green one too,
I like apples, yes I do.

The apples at the market,
I thought I'd like to touch,
They were so smooth and shiny,
I wanted them so much.

Chorus

Then finally at the market,
I sunk my teeth right in,
You should've heard the sound,
(sound...) It made me grin.

Chorus

The apples at the market,
I wanted to taste some more,
I ate the biggest apple,
But I didn't eat the core.

Chorus

And now I go to market,
On an autumn afternoon,
I remember that first day,
I smelled the apple's sweet perfume.

Chorus

Garden Literature

A Day in the Garden: A Picture Book. Bettina Stietencron. 1992. Floris Books, Edinburgh, Scotland. Each picture takes the reader to a new day and a new season in someone's back yard, allowing the reader to imagine a story. As the seasons change, the activities of the family and animals in the garden change too.

Everyday Garden. Cynthia Rylant. 1993. Little Simon, New York, NY. Simple rhyming text rejoices in the perfection of a garden. Colorful illustrations cover two-page spreads, always including a round bug and worm.

Flower Garden. Eve Bunting. 2000. Sandpiper Press, San Anselmo, CA. An African-American girl and her father create a window box for her mother in this lyrical book. Rhyming verse and wonderful, warm illustrations depict a loving family and the joy of growing a flower.

From the Garden: A Counting Book About Growing Food (Know Your Numbers). Michael Dahl. 2004. Picture Window Books, Mankato, MN. Inviting, bright illustrations liven up a potentially dry topic — counting — with the fun of harvesting vegetables to make tossed salad for dinner.

From Seed to Plant. Gail Gibbons. 1993. Holiday House, New York, NY. This simple introduction to plant reproduction includes a detailed section on pollination with clear illustrations, and discusses seed dispersal and growth from seed to plant.

Growing Vegetable Soup. Lois Ehlert. 1991. Harcourt Big Books, New York, NY. Bright pictures show a father and child sharing the simple joy of planting, watering, watching seeds grow, and making the harvest into soup.

Hey Little Ant. Philip Hoose and Hannah Hoose. 2004. Tricycle Press, New York, NY. Based on a song, this narrative describes a boy talking to a tiny ant he wants to squish. The bespectacled ant begs him to reconsider, pointing out that it has a family, too. This delightful parable conveys mercy and empathy, and asks readers to consider life from an insect's point of view.

In the Children's Garden. Carole Lexa Schaefer. 1994. Henry Holt & Co, New York, NY. Young children garden in a community plot in Seattle. Colorful illustrations evoke the unruly yet fertile nature of a youth garden.

Inch by Inch: The Garden Song. David Mallett. 1997. Harper-Collins, New York, NY. A picture-book version of the musician's folksong with gorgeous illustrations. In rhyming text a young gardener plants seeds, tends them, fends off hungry crows, has many adventures, and gathers the harvest. Includes music to the song.

Jack's Garden. Henry Cole. 1997. Greenwillow Books, New York, NY. Delightful text traces a little boy's backyard flower garden from tilling the soil to enjoying the blossoms in a take-off on the old rhyme "This Is the House That Jack Built." Beautiful illustrations show seedlings sprouting, budding, and opening; insects and birds visiting; and finally, a lovely garden in full bloom.

Over in the Garden. Jennifer Ward. 2002. Rising Moon Books, Flagstaff, AZ. This new take on the familiar old counting rhyme features eye-catching garden critters. In bright, bold illustrations, giant insects with large, friendly cartoon-style eyes mingle with larger-than-life flowers, plant stems, and fruits.

Planting a Rainbow. Lois Ehlert. 1992. Voyager Books, New York, NY. This companion book to Ehlert's *Growing Vegetable Soup* celebrates the colorful variety in a flower garden and the cyclical excitement of gardening. In simple sentences, a young child relates the yearly cycle and process of planning, planting, and picking flowers in a garden.

Pumpkin Pumpkin. Jeanne Titherington. 1990. Greenwillow Books, New York, NY. Jamie is a very young gardener. He plants a seed, grows and harvests a pumpkin, and saves seeds for next year. Large, detailed pencil drawings capture Jamie's anticipation and pride. Nonreaders can easily follow the story in pictures alone.

Sunflower House. Eve Bunting. 1999. Voyager Books, New York, NY. In this story about the life cycle a boy plants mammoth sunflowers in a large circle. He waters them, waits as the flowers grow into a perfect sunflower house, plays in it all summer, and collects the seeds for next summer's sunflower house.

Sunflower Sal. Janet S. Anderson. 1999. Albert Whitman & Co, Morton Grove, IL. Sal longs to make a quilt but she just can't sew the tiny stitches. She finds solace — and success — in growing hundreds of sunflowers throughout her village.

Ten Seeds. Ruth Brown. 2001. Knopf, New York, NY. Ten seeds are planted and the countdown begins. Children watch as seeds (then seedlings, shoots, and plants) disappear from various encounters in the garden. The last seed survives, grows into a sunflower, drops 10 new seeds, and the cycle begins again.

The Giant Carrot. Jan Peck. 1998. Dial Publishing, New York, NY. This variation of a Russian folktale about a turnip features a carrot that grows large enough to feed a whole family. The family prepares the soil, plants the seed, and tends the garden, but only the daughter's singing and dancing can make the carrot grow. Includes a recipe for carrot pudding.

The Sun, the Wind, and the Rain. Lisa Westburg Peters. 1990. Henry Holt & Co, New York, NY. As a little girl builds a mountain out of wet sand the author clearly explains the concept of geological mountain formation. Vivid illustrations support this book's simple but accurate scientific information.

The Tiny Seed. Eric Carle. 2009. Little Simon, New York, NY. Carle's trademark collage illustrations beautifully convey the miracle of one tiny seed that grows into a giant flower that eventually releases its seeds to continue the cycle.

What's This? A Seed's Story. Caroline Mockford. 2007. Barefoot Books, Cambridge, MA. One winter morning a little girl finds a seed on the ground. Together with a curious bird and a wise ginger-colored cat, she plants the seed and begins the wondrous process of growing a flower. Exquisite paintings illustrate a flower's life cycle, and the author includes information for adults who may want to go into greater depth with children about roots, shoots, flowers, seeds, and growing sunflowers.

Wonderful Worms. Linda Glaser. 1994. Millbrook Press, Southampton, NY. This informational and engaging nonfiction text for youngsters explains the vital role earthworms play and encourages appreciation for these small creatures. Simple text enables the reader to expand in many directions.

Edible Flowers

This list of edible flowers is just the beginning! While all of the flowers below are edible, only some are palatable. Try a flower before suggesting that your students do the same. Also remember that many plants look alike, so it is essential to read the seed packet or seedling label carefully and ask a professional, such as your local cooperative extension agent, to ensure edibility of an unknown plant.

SUZANNE DEJOHN/NGA

* Anise hyssop
* Apple blossoms — harvest only petals or you will sacrifice future fruit
* Bachelor buttons
* Bee balm
* Borage
* Calendula
* Chamomile
* Citrus blossoms (orange, lemon, lime, grapefruit) — harvest only petals or you will sacrifice future fruit
* Dandelion
* Dill
* Fennel
* Jerusalem sage
* Johnny jump-up
* Lavender
* Lemon balm
* Lemon verbena
* Marigold
* Monarda
* Mustard
* Nasturtium
* Pansy
* Peach blossoms — harvest only petals or you will sacrifice future fruit
* Pear blossoms — harvest only petals or you will sacrifice future fruit
* Pineapple guava blossoms — harvest only petals or you will sacrifice future fruit
* Rose
* Salvia (any salvia)
* Squash blossoms — harvest only male flowers or petals of female flowers, or you will sacrifice future fruit
* Thyme
* Violet

Toxic Garden Plants & Fungi

The following is a list of some common toxic plants. **It is by no means comprehensive.** Before planting anything in a children's garden, check its toxicity with a reliable source, such as your local cooperative extension service.

Ornamentals

* Angel's Trumpet (*Datura* spp.)
* Bleeding heart (*Dicentra formosa*)
* Calla lily (*Zantedeschia aethiopica*)
* Carnation (*Dianthus caryophyllus*)
* Castor-oil plant (*Ricinus communis*)
* Chinese or Japanese lantern (*Physalis*)
* Chrysanthemum
* Clematis
* Crocus (*Colchicum autumnale*)
* Daffodil or jonquil (*Narcissus*)
* Delphinium
* Elderberry
* Elephant's ear (*Diffenbachia*)
* Foxglove (*Digitalis purpurea*)
* Gladiola (bulb)
* Hyacinth (*Hyacinthus orientalis*)
* Iris
* Lily of the valley (*Convallaria*)
* Morning glory (*Ipomaea tricolor*)
* Narcissus
* Pansy, seeds (*Viola tricolor*)
* Peony, root (*Paeonia officinalis*)
* Poinsettia (*Euphorbia*)
* Poison hemlock
* Primrose (*Primula*)
* Sweet pea (*Lathyrus odoratus*)
* Sweet William (*Dianthus barbatus*)
* Tree tobacco (*Nicotiana* spp.)
* Wisteria

Mushrooms

While some mushrooms are edible, many others are extremely toxic and even fatal. Because they are difficult to tell apart, consider all mushrooms in an instructional children's garden off limits for eating.

Vegetable plant parts

* Potato leaves and stems; green patches found on tubers
* Rhubarb leaves
* Tomato leaves and stems

Raw vegetables (fine if cooked)

* Buckwheat (greens)
* Eggplant
* Kidney beans (including sprouts)
* Parsnips
* Potatoes

Hedges, Bushes, and Trees

* Azalea (*Azalea indica*)
* Black locust (*Robinia pseudoacacia*)
* Buckeye
* Buckthorn (*Rhamnus cathartica*)
* Cherry laurel (*Laurocerasus officinalis*)
* Daphne (*Daphne mezereum*)
* Elderberry (not berries)
* Horse chestnut (*Aesculus hippocastanum*)
* Hydrangea
* Laburnum (*Laburnum anagyroides*)
* Oleander (*Nerium oleander*)
* Poison oak, poison ivy
* Privet (*Ligustrum vulgare*)
* Rhododendron
* Virginia creeper (*Ampelopis brevipedunculata*)

SUZANNE DEJOHN/NGA

Preparing In-Ground Garden Beds

If you are starting a new garden in an area that may have toxic substances in the soil, such as an urban, industrial area, have the soil professionally tested for lead or other contaminants. If your soil is toxic, plan to garden in a planter box (see p. 116) filled with a topsoil mix from a local landscape supply company, or make your own, using 5 parts compost, 4 parts garden soil, and 1 part sand.

Preparing the soil. Digging soil when it is too wet or dry damages the soil's structure and makes gardening difficult. Use the "squeeze test" to assess moisture before you break ground. Squeeze a handful of soil into a ball in the palm of your hand. If the ball of soil drips, it's too wet and needs time to dry out. If it falls apart, the soil is too dry and needs to be watered thoroughly. After watering an area, give the water sufficient time to soak into the soil. Repeat the squeeze test until the ball of soil in your hand keeps its shape when you open your hand, but crumbles when lightly tapped. Your soil is now ready for digging.

If your site is small and the ground not too compacted you can turn the soil with spading forks and shovels. But if your site hasn't been gardened recently, chances are the earth is compacted and may be more easily prepared by machine. Rototillers are a good solution for sites less than an acre that have compacted soils or are too large to cultivate by hand. For larger sites, consider using a small tractor with a plowing attachment. You can also use a rototiller to mix in organic matter, cultivate, clear weedy areas, and more.

Staking out the beds. Once your soil is loosened, mark off the garden's perimeter and individual beds with stakes and string. Your planting areas will be cultivated year after year, while the mulched paths will become compacted as people walk on them. For this task, you'll need:

* 18-inch wooden stakes
* Twine or string
* Hammers or mallets
* Measuring tape
* Garden site plan

Pound stakes into the corners of each bed. Make sure the beds are no more than 2 to 3 feet wide, so that small children can reach the middle of the bed while their feet remain on the path. String twine between the stakes to mark the boundaries of each bed and define the area for digging. Allow about three feet between beds so that your pathways are wide enough for a wheelbarrow to pass through and for children to move about and explore their garden with ease.

Digging the garden beds. When establishing new garden beds, we recommend using the double-digging or "French Intensive" method to prepare the beds (see the diagram on the following page). Double digging involves loosening the soil to a depth of 24 inches (or about 2 spades deep) to improve aeration and drainage while adding organic matter to improve the soil's structure and fertility. This method allows roots to grow down rather than out, giving plants access to water and nutrients deep down in the soil. It also reduces the amount of space needed between plants.

If your soil is already loose, as some sandy soils are, then double digging may not be necessary. Double digging is generally used to establish beds and is best done with adult volunteers or older, stronger students. Once you have established beds, their preparation can be as simple as clearing old plant material and weeds, adding a layer of compost, and turning it into the soil with digging forks or hand tools. To shape your bed, simply rake soil from the sides into a mound, and then flatten the top with a rake.

The final step is to mulch the paths. Wood chips from tree pruning companies are an excellent, and often free, source of mulch for paths. Even though the beds are now ready to plant, leave the twine boundaries around them until the garden paths are well established.

Preparing garden beds with young children. You can involve young students in the process of preparing garden beds by letting them dump compost onto the beds from small buckets and dig with hand tools. They may not make much progress but they will get the idea of bed preparation and be delighted to find a worm or two in the process.

DOUBLE DIGGING (SIDE VIEW)

1. Dig out a trench across the width of one end of a bed about 1 foot deep and 1 foot wide. Pile this soil at the end of the bed, not on the bed. This soil will be used later.

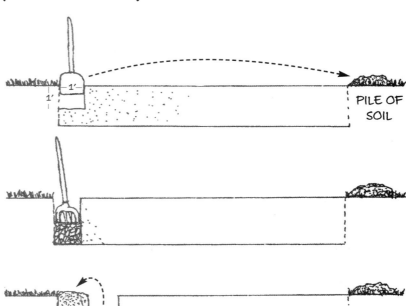

PILE OF SOIL

2. Standing on the untrenched part of the bed, try to dig the digging fork into the trench another 12 inches. Put the fork down as far as it will go and "wiggle" it, trying to loosen the subsoil, but not remove it. Do this across the entire trench.

3. Dig another trench behind the first one. This time, use this soil to fill the first trench. Remember: Trenches should only be 1 foot wide.

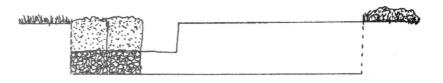

4. Then, loosen the subsoil.

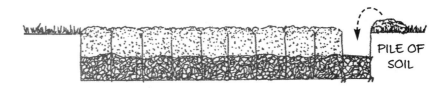

5. Continue along the bed ...

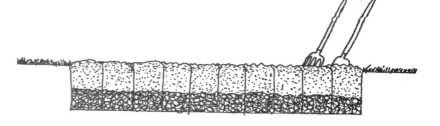

6. ... until it is completed. When you have emptied the very last trench and loosened the subsoil, fill that trench with the soil you laid aside from the first trench.

PILE OF SOIL

THE FINISHED PRODUCT.

Seed Starting and Transplanting

(Adapted with permission from the National Gardening Association)

Some seeds grow best when started in small containers and later transplanted into the garden bed, while others grow best when sown directly in the garden. Consult the Vegetable Planting Guide (p. 98) or the back of your seed packets to determine which method is best for the seeds you plan to sow.

Scheduling/Planning

Your first challenge is to determine when you want to have seedlings (baby plants) ready to give away, sell, or plant outdoors. To develop a planting calendar, you'll need to know:

* the average last spring frost date in your area (visit *www.victoryseeds.com/frost/index.html*, check with local gardeners or nurseries, or your county's Cooperative Extension Service);
* the time required from sowing each type of seed to transplanting it outdoors (check seed packets);
* the time from seed sowing to harvest ("days to harvest") if you want to harvest at a particular time, such as a spring harvest before school gets out or a fall harvest as students return to school.

Good resources to help you develop a planting calendar include seed packets, seed catalogs, and this book's Vegetable Planting Guide.

Supplies

Containers. Many types of containers will work, as long as they're at least 2 to 3 inches deep and have drainage holes. Try using nursery 6-packs, old yogurt containers, the bottom halves of milk cartons, and homemade newspaper pots (see sidebar, p. 96).

Soil. Start seedlings in a seed-starting mix — it holds water and is light; commercial mixes are also weed free and sterile. You can buy a commercial mix or make your own using 5 parts compost, 4 parts garden soil, and 1 part sand.

Light. Although you can grow seedlings on windowsills that get plenty of light (south-facing windows are best), they tend to be "leggy." Seedlings grow best with 14 to 16 hours of light a day, much more than most windows supply, especially in winter. You'll get better results using fluorescent lights. To prevent stretched, leggy stems, keep the lights within a few inches of the top leaves.

Planting and Maintenance

Planting. Before planting, wet the soil mix completely so that it is as moist as a wrung-out sponge. Fill containers, then tap them to settle the soil without packing it too tightly. A good rule of thumb is to plant seeds two to three times as deep as they are wide. A few types of seeds either require light to germinate (check the seed package) or are so small that you should press them gently into the top of the soil without covering them. Be sure to keep the soil surrounding germinating seeds moist (not soggy). If the surface of your soil mix tends to dry quickly, probe to the depth of the seed or young roots to check for moistness below the surface. To help maintain soil moisture, try covering the containers with waxed paper or a light fabric and gently sprinkle the seedlings regularly so they don't dry out (a spray bottle works well in the classroom).

Pricking out. If you saved space by planting many seeds in a container or flat, you will have to move or "prick" them out to individual containers with more space. Once the first true leaves appear (after the cotyledons), gently tease out closely planted seedlings with a pencil point, popsicle stick, or butter knife and transplant them to individual containers. Lift seedlings by their cotyledons or leaves rather than by their lifeline: the stem.

Tending seedlings. It's best to water seedlings when they need it rather than on a regular schedule. Have students test soil moisture with a finger, and water only when the top half inch of soil is dry. You can begin fertilizing seedlings once their first true leaves appear, but be careful not to overdo it. The right amount of organic fertilizer will help keep your seedlings looking dark green (rather than pale yellow). Students may want to experiment to discover for themselves the difference between seedlings raised with and without fertilizer.

Hardening off. Before moving seedlings outdoors, "harden" them off to get them accustomed to harsher outdoor conditions. Do this by setting seedlings outside for progressively longer periods each day, starting with a few hours and increasing to a full day over the course of a week or so. Your students may want to experiment to see how the health and growth of a hardened-off plant compares with one transplanted directly outside.

What to transplant, and when. Not all plants do well when started in containers. For example, root crops such as carrots, radishes, and beets don't transplant well and should not be started in containers. The best candidates for an early indoor start are those plants that tolerate root disturbance and that benefit from a jump on the season. You can start and set out cool-weather crops like broccoli, cauliflower, and cabbage up to a month before the last danger of frost in your area. Transplant warm-weather crops like tomatoes, peppers, and melons after all danger of frost is past in your area. Planting requirements vary for flowers, so check the seed packets.

Tips for transplanting. Your seedlings are ready for transplanting when they have at least two sets of true leaves and their root systems are established enough to hold soil around them. Transplant to moist (not soggy) garden soil. Refer to the Vegetable Planting Guide or seed packet to determine the appropriate spacing. If your

transplants are rootbound, with a large mass of roots at the bottom of the plant, gently break up the rootball before transplanting. Transplant seedlings to the same depth that they were in their containers. Water transplants using many passes of gentle sprays, letting the water seep into the soil between passes, or trickle water directly onto the soil around the plant's root zone until the water has percolated to the root depth. Use your finger to make sure the soil is wet to the depth of the roots (often students stop watering when only the surface is wet). Avoid transplanting during midday heat. Protect your transplants from pests such as birds by covering the young plants with upside down strawberry baskets, netting, or floating row covers (thin, lightweight fabrics).

Involving young students. For ideas on how to involve your young students in seed starting and trans-

---

Make Your Own Paper Pots

It's easy to make paper pots that can be transplanted directly into the garden. The basic idea is to wrap a newspaper strip around a mold, fold in the bottom, fill it with soil, and then plant a seed in it.

Materials:

❀ Potmaker. You can either purchase a two-part wooden mold or use a 5.5 oz juice can. Potmaker molds are available from the National Gardening Association (*www.gardeningwithkids.org*). The hardwood molds are extremely durable and students love to make pots with them.

❀ Newspaper

❀ Bag of seed-starting mix

❀ Nursery tray or container to hold and support paper pots. We like using milk cartons cut in half lengthwise.

Instructions

❀ Cut 3" x 10" strips of newspaper.

❀ Place a strip of newspaper lengthwise in front of you, then place the mold at the bottom end of the paper strip so you can roll it along the strip. Leave about 1 1/2 inches of width hanging over the bottom of the mold.

❀ Roll the mold along the strip, wrapping the paper around it. When you reach the end of the strip, twist and fold the extra paper at the bottom onto itself.

❀ The wooden mold has a matching bottom piece. If using it, place the top onto the bottom piece and twist and press. If using a juice can, twist and press the bottom as tightly as possible. Use your thumbs to press the paper firmly into the indent in the bottom of the can, all the way around.

❀ Gently ease the newspaper "pot" off its mold. Fill it to the top with soil, poke a hole in the soil with your index finger, plant a seed, and cover it.

❀ Place pots closely together in a tray so that they can support each other.

❀ Water carefully.

❀ If children plan to take their pots home, put them in a small container. For a sturdier pot, use regular office copy paper instead of newspaper. When the plant is 3 to 5 inches tall, transplant it into the ground, pot and all. Cover the pot completely with soil, so that exposed paper doesn't wick moisture away from the pot and keep it from decomposing.

Watering Tips

(Adapted from "Water Conservation Tips," by Martha Brown, University of California, Santa Cruz.

Many factors determine the right time to water your garden. Soil type, recent weather, root depths, and whether your plants are newly transplanted or well established are all factors to consider. The best way to determine immediate need is to use the squeeze test to assess the moisture in your soil. Dig down a few inches, grab a handful of soil, and squeeze it into a ball. If no ball forms, water right away. If a few gentle taps to the ball breaks it up, think about watering soon. If the ball sticks tight or oozes, wait to water.

Soil type often dictates how often to water your garden. Clay soils drain slowly and can hold water for up to two weeks; sandy soils drain quickly, holding water for only a few days. Adding compost to any type of soil will assist in its water-holding capacity. For clay soils, compost improves drainage and opens up air spaces so that roots can breathe. Compost added to sandy soils acts like a sponge, absorbing and retaining moisture until plants can use it. When it's time to irrigate, here are some water-saving guidelines:

Deep waterings that wet the entire root zone use water most effectively. The goal is to draw plant roots deep into the soil, where water remains available longer. If all the moisture remains in the top few inches of the bed, that's where the roots will stay, and shallow-rooted plants are especially vulnerable to drying out. Deep waterings combined with deeply dug soil encourage roots to spread and lengthen. An exception: don't let newly planted seed beds and young transplants dry out — the germinating seeds or seedling roots are near the soil surface, which needs to stay moist. As the plants mature and their roots lengthen, they can tolerate longer intervals between waterings.

Watering with young children. A great way to involve all children in watering is to provide one big bucket of water and many small cups. Have children fill their cup, walk it to a bed and pour, and then return for more. This helps to prevent any one student from overwatering, as can happen with a watering can or hose. Make sure an adult supervises the bucket of water at all times, and empty it when you leave the garden.

Mulch Slows Evaporation

Anything that covers the ground and blocks light can act as a mulch. This includes inorganic material such as plastic sheeting, polypropylene or polyester landscape fabrics, and old carpet. Organic mulches range from compost, leaves, straw, and hay, to newspaper, wood chips, bark, and sawdust. Mulching tips:

* ❋ Don't layer organic mulch so densely that it forms an impenetrable barrier — water should be able to pass through to the soil. Clay soils need a thinner mulch layer than sandy soils.
* ❋ Leave the area near the plant stem or tree trunk unmulched to allow air to circulate.
* ❋ Leaves, grass clippings (mixed with other material to keep them from matting), straw, or hay make a good mulch for most plants.
* ❋ Don't overuse resinous materials such as redwood bark or eucalyptus, since these can eventually become toxic to the plants.
* ❋ Straw mulches are especially effective under well-established tomato, squash, and melon plants. They cool the soil, slow evaporation, and keep the fruit from making contact with wet soil.
* ❋ Because mulch keeps the soil surface moist, roots tend to stay closer to the surface. Use mulch consistently throughout the summer and early fall to prevent these shallower roots from drying out. Remove it as the weather cools to help the soil stay warm.

Some gardeners add a layer of diatomaceous earth or rock powder beneath mulch to discourage soft-bodied pests. If pests persist, you may have to restrict mulching efforts to less-vulnerable plants. Rather than mulching, try digging compost or decomposed leaves into the top few inches of soil to improve its water-holding capacity.

Consider Drip Irrigation

Landscape and gardening stores offer an array of water-conserving irrigation systems, often lumped under the heading of "drip irrigation." These range from soaker hoses that attach to regular garden hoses to automated systems that incorporate programmable timers to water individual beds or plants on a preset sequence. The idea is to conserve water by directing it to the base of the plants, where it's most needed. Drip irrigation also limits weed growth and, by keeping the foliage dry, it helps control mildew and fungus problems as well.

A drip irrigation system coupled with a timer is a great aid in maintaining school gardens during summer and other vacation times. Consult your garden center for the best system for your garden.

Vegetable Planting Guide

Vegetable	Warm weather	Cool weather	Sow in container	Sow direct	SPRING PLANTING		FALL PLANTING
					Start seeds indoors (weeks before last frost)	Plant seeds or transplants outdoors (weeks before or after last frost)	Weeks before 1st frost
Beans, bush	•			•		1-2 after	12 before
Beans, pole	•			•		1-2 after	12 before
Beets	•	•		•		2-4 before	8-10 before
Broccoli		•	•		4-6 before	4-6 before	14-17 before
Brussels sprouts		•	•		5-8 before	4-6 before	17 before
Cabbage	•	•	•		4-6 before	5 before	13-14 before
Carrots	•	•		•		2-4 before	13 before
Cauliflower		•	•		5-8 before	1-2 before	14 before
Celery	•	•	•		8-10 before	2-3 before	19 before
Chard	•	•	•		2-4 before	1-2 before	6 before
Corn	•			•		1-2 after	6 before
Cucumber	•		•	•	2-3 before	1-2 after	11$\frac{1}{2}$ before
Eggplant	•		•		6-8 before	2-3 after	14 before
Garlic		•		•		6 before	Sept.-Nov. with mulch
Kale		•	•		5-8 before	5 before	6-8 before
Kohlrabi		•	•		3-4 before	2-3 before	10 before
Leeks		•	•		8-10 before	3-4 before	6-8 before
Lettuce	•	•	•	•	3-4 before	2-4 before; 3 after	6-8 before
Onions		•	•	•	8-10 before	3 before; 2 after	depends on variety
Parsley	•	•	•	•	4-6 before	1-2 after	8-10 before
Peas		•		•		4-6 before; 2-3 after	12 before
Peppers	•		•		6-8 before	1-3 after	
Potatoes	•			•		1-2 before	
Pumpkins	•			•		after frost	
Radishes	•	•		•		4-6 before	7 before
Spinach		•		•		3-6 before	6-8 before
Squash, summer	•		•	•	2-3 before	1-4 after	10 before
Squash, winter	•			•		2 after	13 before
Tomatoes	•		•		4-5 before	2-4 after	

Vegetable	Days to emerge	Days to harvest	Spacing of plants (inches)	Depth to plant seeds (inches)	Soil temp. for germination (degrees F)	Best air temp. for growing (degrees F)
Beans, bush	4-10	50-60	6	1	60-85	60-80
Beans, pole	4-10	60-70	6-8	1	60-85	60-80
Beets	7-10	50-75	2-4	$1/2$	60-75	50-75
Broccoli	5-10	60-75	15-18	$1/4$	60-75	55-70
Brussels sprouts	8-10	100-110	18	$1/4$	65-75	55-70
Cabbage	4-10	60-100	18	$1/4$	60-75	50-75
Carrots	10-17	60-80	2	$1/4$	55-75	45-75
Cauliflower	5-10	60-70	15-18	$1/4$	60-75	60-72
Celery	7-12	70-100	6	$1/4$	60-75	60-75
Chard	4-14	45-55	8-12	1	50-70	45-75
Corn	3-10	50-100	12-15	1	55-85	60-95
Cucumber	3-8	60-80	12-24	1	65-85	60-80
Eggplant	5-13	90	12-18	$1/2$	65-85	65-85
Garlic	10-15	90-120	4-6	$1/2$	45-65	40-65
Kale	5-10	55-70	12-15	$1/2$	40-70	40-70
Kohlrabi	5-10	50-70	6-9	$1/4$	50-75	40-75
Leeks	7-14	80-160	4-6	$1/2$	below 70	50-70
Lettuce	4-10	45-70	10-12	$1/4$	45-70	55-70
Onions	4-12	60-90	4-6	$1/4$	50-80	60-85
Parsley	11-25	70-90	6	$1/4$	50-85	60-65
Peas	6-15	60-80	4	1	40-75	55-75
Peppers	8-20	80-100	10-12	$1/2$	65-90	65-85
Potatoes	10-15	70-100	10-12	6	60-65	60-80
Pumpkins	7-10	90-130	36	1	65-85	50-90
Radishes	3-10	25-40	1-2	$1/4$	40-85	45-75
Spinach	6-14	40-55	4-8	$1/4$	50-70	40-75
Squash, summer	3-12	60-85	15-24	1	65-85	60-85
Squash, winter	4-10	80-120	24-36	$1/2$ to 1	65-85	60-85
Tomatoes	6-14	65-90	18-24	$1/4$ to $1/2$	65-85	65-85

Companion Planting Guides

(Adapted from a variety of sources)

Farmers and gardeners have experimented with planting plants in combination for better crop success. We've listed some commonly accepted plant companions below. Your students can experiment to see if they notice higher yield, better flavor, fewer pest problems, etc., when they plant plants in combination as compared with a control crop.

HERB	COMPANIONS AND EFFECTS
Basil	Companion to tomatoes; dislikes rue intensely; improves growth and flavor; repels mosquitoes and flies.
Bee balm	Companion to tomatoes; improves growth and flavor.
Borage	Companion to tomatoes, squash, and strawberries; deters tomato worms; improves flavor and growth.
Catnip	Plant in borders; deters flea beetles.
Chamomile	Companion to cabbage and onions; improves growth and flavor.
Chervil	Companion to radishes; improves growth and flavor.
Chives	Companion to carrots; improves growth and flavor; plant around base of fruit trees to discourage insects climbing trunks.
Dill	Companion to cabbage; dislikes carrots; improves growth and health of cabbage.
Fennel	Plant away from the garden; most plants dislike it.
Garlic	Plant near roses and raspberries; improves growth and health; deters Japanese beetles; plant liberally throughout garden to deter pests.
Horseradish	Plant at corners of potato patch to deter potato bugs.
Lamb's quarters	Allow this edible weed to grow in moderate amounts in the garden, especially in the corn patch.
Lemon balm	Sprinkle throughout the garden.
Marigolds	The workhorse of the pest deterrents; plant throughout the garden, especially with tomatoes; it discourages Mexican bean beetles, nematodes, and other insects.
Mint	Companion to cabbage and tomatoes; improves health and flavor; deters white cabbage moths.
Marjoram	Plant here and there in the garden; improves flavor.
Nasturtium	Companion to tomatoes and cucumbers.
Petunia	Protects beans; beneficial throughout the garden.
Purslane	This edible weed makes a good ground cover in the corn patch.
Pigweed	One of the best weeds for pumping nutrients from the subsoil, it is especially beneficial to potatoes, onions, and corn; keep weeds thinned.
Rosemary	Companion to cabbage, beans, carrots, and sage; deters cabbage moths, bean beetles, and carrot flies.
Rue	Keep it far away from sweet basil; plant near roses and raspberries; deters Japanese beetles.
Sage	Plant with rosemary, cabbage, carrots, beans, and peas; keep away from cucumbers; deters cabbage moths and carrot flies.
Summer savory	Plant with beans and onions; improves growth and flavor; deters bean beetles.
Tarragon	Good throughout the garden.
Thyme	Plant here and there in the garden; it deters cabbage worms.
Yarrow	Plant along borders, paths, near aromatic herbs; enhances essential oil production.

VEGETABLE	PLANT WITH	DON'T PLANT WITH
Beans	Potatoes, carrots, cucumbers, cauliflower, cabbage, summer savory, most other vegetables and herbs	Onion, garlic, gladiolus
Beans, bush	Potatoes, cucumbers, corn, celery, summer savory, sunflowers, strawberries	Onions
Beans, pole	Cabbage, carrots, corn, cucumbers, summer savory	Onions, beets
Beets	Onions, cabbage	Pole beans
Cabbage family (cabbage, cauliflower, kale, kohlrabi, broccoli)	Aromatic plants, potatoes, celery, dill, chamomile, sage, peppermint, rosemary, beets, onions, thyme, lavender, bush beans	Strawberries, tomatoes, pole beans
Carrots	Peas, leaf lettuce, chives, onions, leeks, rosemary, sage, tomatoes	Dill
Celery	Leeks, tomatoes, bush beans, cucumbers	
Corn	Potatoes, peas, beans, cucumbers, squash, pumpkins	
Cucumbers	Beans, corn, peas, radishes, sunflowers	Potatoes, aromatic herbs
Eggplant	Beans	
Leeks	Onions, celery, carrots	
Lettuce	Carrots and radishes (lettuce, carrots, and radishes make a strong team grown together), strawberries, cucumbers	
Onions/Garlic	Beets, strawberries, tomatoes, lettuce, summer savory, chamomile	Peas
Parsley	Tomatoes, asparagus	
Peas	Carrots, turnips, radishes, cucumbers, corn, beans, most vegetables, herbs (adds nitrogen to soil)	Onions, garlic, gladiolus, potatoes
Potatoes	Beans, corn, cabbage, horseradish (should be planted at corners of patch), marigolds, eggplant (as a lure for Colorado potato beetles)	Pumpkins, squash, cucumbers, sunflowers, tomatoes
Pumpkins	Corn	Potatoes
Radishes	Peas, nasturtiums, lettuce, cucumbers	
Spinach	Strawberries	
Squash	Nasturtiums, corn	
Strawberries	Bush beans, lettuce	
Tomatoes	Chives, onions, parsley, asparagus, marigolds, nasturtiums, carrots, lima beans	Kohlrabi, potatoes, fennel, cabbage family
Turnips	Peas	

Vegetable Planting and Harvesting Tips

Beans, bush: Sow every 2 weeks for a constant supply of beans. Plants may stop producing beans during extreme heat but will begin again when temperatures decrease. Pick before you can see bean seeds swelling in the pods, and pick frequently (every 3 to 5 days) so the crop keeps producing. Sensitive to transplanting, best sown directly in garden. Eat raw, steamed, boiled, or pickled in vinegar.

Beans, pole: A climbing bean that needs the support of a pole, trellis, or fence to grow. Pole beans often produce for a longer period than other beans. Pick before you can see bean seeds swelling in the pods, and pick frequently (every 3 to 5 days) for continual harvest. Sensitive to transplanting, best sown directly in garden. Eat raw, steamed, boiled, or pickled in vinegar.

Beans, shelling: These beans grow until both the beans and pods have completely dried on the plant. Place the harvested dried bean pods on a tarp and have students stomp on them to remove the pods, or place shells in a sack and strike the sack to break beans from shells. Some kids like to hand shell each pod. Cook these beans prior to eating.

Beets: Sow seed directly in the garden every 10 days for continual harvest. Thin plants when they are young. Harvest when beets are 1 to 2 1/2 inches in diameter; they become woody when overmature. Beet roots survive light frosts in the ground. Eat roots raw, pureed, marinated, stewed, or pickled in vinegar; cook greens as you would spinach.

Broccoli: This cool-season crop grows best in full sun. Pick broccoli when heads form into tight, firm clusters. Cut off the head with 6 inches of stem attached. Side heads will form after the first head is cut. Eat florets and stems raw, boiled, or steamed.

Brussels Sprouts: Plant in spring for a fall harvest. Exposure to frost improves flavor and sweetness. To harvest, twist sprouts off the stem when 1 1/2 inches in diameter; start with lower ones first. Remaining sprouts will keep on plants through part of the winter. Eat boiled, steamed, or baked.

CHILD'S PLAY EARLY LEARNING CENTER, INC.

Cabbage: Plant in midsummer for a fall harvest. In mild areas, sow in fall for an early spring harvest. Harvest when cabbages have formed tight, firm heads. Eat raw, boiled, steamed, or pickled as sauerkraut.

Carrots: Sow seed directly in the garden. Thin crowded plants when small. Harvest at almost any time in the growth cycle. Carrots will keep in the garden after the first frost, right up until the ground freezes in winter. If needed, loosen carrots with a digging fork before pulling. Eat raw, boiled, baked, pureed, or pickled in vinegar.

Cauliflower: This cool-season crop does best if you tie the outer leaves around the heads to protect them from the sun. Harvest heads once the florets are tightly formed and dense. Cut the head off the main stem. Eat raw, steamed, boiled, or pureed.

Celery: Requires a lot of nutrients and water. Harvest once the stalks are 12 inches or longer. The inner stalks are more tender and taste best uncooked.

Chard: Cut outer leaves close to the ground when 8 to 10 inches tall, leaving four to six leaves on the plant so it can continue to grow. Refrigerate chard for up to two weeks. Cook by boiling, steaming, or stir-frying.

Corn (sweet): Sensitive to transplanting; best sown directly in the garden. For good pollination, plant in blocks at least 4 feet square. Ears are ready to harvest about 20 days after the silks appear or when silks turn brown. Peel back the husk and puncture a kernel with your fingernail. If the kernels are fat with milky white juice, the ear is ready to harvest. Eat raw, steamed, or boiled.

Corn (pop): Sensitive to transplanting; best sown directly in the garden. Do not plant sweet corn and popcorn in the same garden; the quality of the sweet corn deteriorates if cross-pollinated by popcorn. Allow popcorn kernels to dry in the field as long as possible before winter rains. Harvest when kernels are hard and the husks dry. Remove the husks and place the ears in mesh bags and hang in a warm, dry location. Once a week, shell a few kernels and try popping them; when test kernels are popping well, store ears in a cool, dark, dry place or remove kernels and store in airtight containers.

Cucumbers: Mound soil into hills; plant 3 seeds per hill. Try growing cucumbers vertically on a trellis to increase air circulation and sunlight. Cucumbers are tastiest when harvested young before the seeds fully develop. Harvest lemon cucumbers when they are light green with just a blush of lemon color. Eat raw.

Eggplant: In northern gardens with short growing seasons, start with transplants. Eggplant may develop a

ALICIA DICKERSON/LIFE LAB

bitter flavor when grown in stressful conditions. Pick fruits while the skins are glossy and before seeds form inside. Cut the stem, rather than pulling it from the plant. Before cooking, salt the eggplant and let it sit for 15 minutes. Then rinse in water to reduce bitterness. Eat baked, pureed, stuffed, or roasted.

Garlic: Harvest when half to three-quarters of the leaves turn yellow-brown. Remove the flower stalks to encourage efficient bulb growth. Loosen the soil beneath the bulb before pulling it. Tie garlic together in bundles of six to ten bulbs and hang them for four to six weeks in a shaded, dry area to cure. Mince and use in any dish as flavoring.

Kale: Pluck the outside leaves when they are 10 inches or longer. To keep the plants producing, avoid cutting the center bud or leaves. Frost enhances the flavor. Eat pureed, boiled, steamed, or baked in a casserole.

Kohlrabi: For the best texture, harvest kohlrabi bulbs when they reach 2 to 3 inches in diameter. Bulbs become tougher as they grow and age. Pull or slice bulbs at their base. The bulbous stem and leaves are edible. Peel bulbs before eating. Eat raw, steamed, boiled, or pureed.

Leeks: Transplant seedlings when 4 inches high. Harvest leeks when they are 1 inch in diameter and before they make a flower stalk. Slice them open lengthwise and rinse the inner leaves. Eat in soups, salads, baked dishes, or as a substitute for chives.

Lettuce: Lettuce prefers cool weather. In hot weather it may go to seed (or bolt) prematurely. Harvest outer leaves of leaf lettuce early to encourage growth. Harvest head lettuce when heads are firm and tight.

Melons: Sensitive to transplanting; best sown directly in the garden. Melons grow best in hot weather. Harvesting a perfectly ripe melon isn't always easy; refer to seed packet information for particular varieties. Eat right in the garden for ultimate satisfaction.

Cantaloupes: Pick when heavy and tan. Look for "netting" that is hard and raised, and a crack that forms around the stem where it touches the fruit. The stem should slip easily off the vine with a quick pull, but should not have fallen off by itself.

Honeydews: Should have a slight yellow blush and get a bit softer at the blossom end.

Watermelons: Develop a dull green cast and have a light patch at the bottom that changes from green to light yellow when mature. Also, the leaf on the tendril nearest the fruit turns brown and withers. The skin should be hard — difficult to pierce with a fingernail.

Onions: Harvest when tops fall over and tips of leaves start to turn brown. Pull onions, shake off any

soil, but do not wash them or remove the outer leaves. Store onions in a dry area to cure for about a week. Use raw, blanched, boiled, baked, or sautéed.

Parsley: Long germination and growth period. Soak seeds overnight before planting. Start harvesting parsley as soon as plants are growing vigorously. Snip outer stems from plants; they will produce new growth. Parsley dries and freezes well. Eat fresh or in soups and baked dishes.

Peas: Sensitive to transplanting; best sown directly in the garden. Harvest peas daily to encourage vines to keep producing. Eat raw, boiled, steamed, or stir-fried.

Peas, shelling: Pick when the pods are rounded and the peas have filled in the pod, but before they grow tough. Pods are not edible.

Peas, snap: Pick when the edible pods begin to grow rounded, plump, and juicy, but before they get tough.

Peas, snow: Pick when the pods have grown to 2 to 3 inches but are still flat.

Peppers: Sensitive to cold and harsh sun. In extreme heat, shade peppers by planting in a dense block. Peppers are edible when they're green, but most don't develop full flavor and mineral content until they turn from green to orange, yellow, or red. Eat raw, boiled, baked, stuffed, or stir-fried.

Potatoes: Tubers are ready to harvest a couple of weeks after the foliage starts to wither and die. Let the soil dry out a bit to help cure the potato skins. Dig with a spading fork before the first frost. Do not wash potatoes before storing them; simply brush off the dirt. Store potatoes in a dark place. Potatoes that are nicked or bruised during harvest don't store well, so eat these tubers as soon as possible. Harvest "new potatoes" before the plant begins to die back. Wash and enjoy

new potatoes shortly after harvest. Always cook potatoes, the raw starch is mostly indigestible. Boil, steam, or bake. Leaves are not edible.

Pumpkins: Direct sow three to four seeds per hill. Leave plenty of room for vines to sprawl (6 feet for bush types and 10 to 12 feet between vining sorts). Do not pick pumpkins until the vine begins to turn brown and dry. Then cut vines 3 to 4 inches above pumpkins. Leave pumpkins in the sun for a week or two to cure. Eat baked, boiled, or pureed. It is easiest to remove pumpkin flesh from skin after cooking.

Radishes: Sow seeds directly in the garden every 10 days for continual harvest. Spring radishes mature quickly so check roots frequently; they become woody when overmature. Pull roots when they are 1 to 2 inches in diameter. Eat raw, stir-fried, or pickled in vinegar.

Spinach: Sensitive to transplanting; best sown directly in the garden. Plant every two weeks for a continual harvest. Harvest larger outer leaves early in the morning when they are crisp. Or, cut whole plants at the base. Keep growing plants cool — they will go to seed (bolt) in hot weather. Wash leaves well and eat raw, pureed, stir-fried, steamed, boiled, or in baked dishes.

Squash, summer: Sensitive to transplanting; best sown directly in the garden. Pick frequently when fruits are small. Skins should be tender enough to poke a fingernail through. Pick zucchini no larger than 6 to 7 inches, patty pan squash at 2 to 3 inches, and round zucchini at 3 to 4 inches. There is no need to peel summer squash. Eat raw, boiled, baked, roasted, or in soups.

Squash, winter: Sensitive to transplanting; best sown directly in the garden. Grow throughout the season and harvest when plants die back in fall and squash skins are hard. Most winter squashes store well. After harvest, store in a cool, dry place. Eat boiled, baked, or pureed in soups. It is easiest to remove squash flesh from the skin after cooking.

Tomatoes: This crop prefers warm weather, although nighttime temperatures over 90 degrees can prevent fruiting. Harvest when fruits are full color. Eat raw, stuffed, stewed, boiled, baked, or pureed. Leaves are not edible. This is a great crop to compare the taste of fresh versus store-bought fruits.

You can find more information on planting and harvesting vegetables at: *www.burpee.com*, *www.garden.org*, *http://gardening.about.com*, *www.organicgardening.com*, and *www.reneesgarden.com*.

Year-Round Garden and Planning Tasks

(Adapted with permission from the UC Davis Children's Garden Program)

This guide is meant to provide general suggestions for a selection of plantings and garden tasks. Planting and garden tasks vary greatly based on climatic zones. Refer to your county's Cooperative Extension office, regional planting guides, or nursery centers for specific suggestions for your area.

	FALL SEPT, OCT, NOV	WINTER DEC, JAN, FEB	SPRING MAR, APR, MAY	SUMMER JUNE, JULY, AUG
Garden tasks through the seasons	• Inventory tools • Weed garden paths and open areas; cover these in deep layers of wood chips or other path material • Mulch cold-sensitive perennials • Save seeds of summer flowers or warm-season crops • Collect plant material and make compost piles • Sow cover crops • Plant perennial flowers and shrubs • In cold areas, protect plants from frost	• Prune trees and shrubs • Cut back dead flower stalks on perennial herbs and ornamentals • Add compost and mulch to the base of fruit trees and perennials • Cover frost-sensitive plants • Order seeds and plan your spring garden • Stay ahead of winter weeds • Maintain worm compost bins • Put out bird feeders • Make or check plant labels	• Flush and repair irrigation systems • Treat any insect pest problems that arise • Remove dead flowers to keep new blossoms coming • Apply mulch to perennials that need it for protection against summer heat • Mulch annuals you want to maintain through summer • Flip or make compost • Protect seedlings from birds with netting or row covers • Protect seedlings from late frost with row covers	• Set up watering schedule • Water and weed • Remove dead flowers to keep new blossoms coming • Save seeds • Make a plan for fall perennial plantings of herbs, native plants, habitat gardens, etc. • Enjoy the harvest
Planting options	**Annuals:** beets, broccoli, cabbage, carrots, cauliflower, chard, fava beans, garlic, kale, lettuce, onions, peas, potatoes, radishes, spinach, wheat, annual flowers (bachelor buttons, calendula, sweet peas, wildflower seed), spring-flowering bulbs (daffodils, lilies, tulips, etc.) **Perennials:** herbs, native plants, ornamentals	**Annuals** (in mild winter areas): broccoli, cabbage, cauliflower, chard, kale, lettuce, peas, spinach **Perennials** (in mild winter areas): bare-root fruit trees and cane fruits such as blackberries and raspberries	**Annuals:** annual flowers, beans, beets, broccoli, cabbage, carrots, cauliflower, chard, cucumbers, eggplant, onions, peppers, potatoes, summer squash, tomatoes **Perennials:** habitat plants, herbs, native plants, ornamentals; in harsh winter areas plant bare-root trees and fruiting vines	**Annuals (plant in early summer):** annual flowers, basil, beans, corn (ornamental, pop, sweet), cucumbers, dill, eggplant, gourds, melons, peppers, pumpkins, summer squash, tomatoes, winter squash
Harvest options	**From previous seasons:** basil, corn (ornamental, pop, sweet), dry beans, eggplant, gourds, late potatoes, melons, okra, peppers, pumpkins, soy beans, summer squash, sunflower seeds, sunflowers, tomatoes, winter squash **From this season:** baby beets, baby carrots, broccoli, cauliflower, chard, lettuce, peas, potatoes, radishes, spinach **Perennials:** apples, grapes, kiwis, pears, persimmons, pomegranates	**From previous seasons:** beets, broccoli, cabbage, carrots, cauliflower, chard, kale, lettuce, peas, potatoes, radishes, spinach **Perennials** (in mild winter areas): citrus	**From previous seasons:** broccoli, chard, fava beans, garlic, kale, lettuce, onions, peas, spinach, wheat **From this season:** carrots, chard, kale, lettuce, potatoes, spinach **Perennials:** artichokes, asparagus, berries, cherries	**From previous seasons:** annual flowers, basil, beans, beets, carrots, eggplant, peppers, potatoes, summer squash, sweet corn, tomatoes **From this season:** basil, tomatoes **Perennials:** various fruiting trees and vines

Composting

ALICIA DICKERSON/LIFE LAB

Healthy plants grow in healthy soil. When you build and maintain fertile soil rich in organic matter, you literally lay the groundwork for thriving plants that can develop quickly, resist pests and diseases, and yield a bountiful crop.

Each time you harvest crops or pull weeds, you make a "withdrawal" from the soil's pool of nutrients and organic matter; if these aren't replaced, the soil is eventually robbed of the resources plants need to flourish. Organic matter in the form of compost can help replenish nutrients and at the same time improve soil structure, making it easier to work and a more hospitable place for plants to thrive.

Composting Defined

Compost is a mixture of decomposed vegetation that is used to improve soil structure and provide plants with necessary nutrients for growth and development. Composting is the art of ecologically reusing waste. When making a compost pile, we are mimicking the nutrient cycle in nature. We are promoting the biological decomposition of organic matter under controlled conditions and demonstrating the concept of cycles and changes. In addition, we are showing our students a way to divert waste headed to landfills.

Decomposition is the result of the efforts of billions of microorganisms, mainly bacteria and fungi, which eat the organic matter and in so doing break it into smaller, simpler molecules that become available as nutrients for plants. As they eat their way through the compost, they give off heat. This heat speeds the decomposition process and can be felt and measured by students.

Compost allows students to see that what we call waste may be nutrients in disguise. You can add organic matter (food wastes, weeds, leaves, manure) to the compost pile and retrieve it a few months later as valuable fertilizer. Composting gives students an opportunity to experience the nutrient cycle and create abundant fertilizer that builds the garden soil — and it's free!

Composting Methods

There are two basic methods for making compost: one is fast and the other slow. The fast method produces compost in three to four months. You build an entire pile and then turn it every few days, so that the outside of the old pile becomes the inside of the new pile. This technique speeds up the decomposition process. It is labor-intensive, involves collecting a large amount of material all at once, and is not always advisable for school gardens, unless you have plenty of time and energy to keep turning your pile. The slow method, which takes 6 to 12 months to produce a useable product, is often more applicable in school gardens. Using this technique, you build a layered pile of organic matter, and leave it to decompose until it is ready for use in the garden. You can also build a compost pile over time, adding layer by layer as materials become available.

Collecting Materials

Traditionally, compost is made in the fall when there is an abundant supply of dried materials. However, building compost piles throughout the year will provide your garden with compost year-round. The more materials you gather, the more compost you can make. You may want to schedule a school-wide composting day and gather materials in advance. Most decomposable materials are useable. Good examples include kitchen vegetable scraps, crop wastes, and straw. **Do not include:** feces from meat-eating animals, animal parts, noxious weeds, plants with resins, meat or fish, greasy foods, or toxic materials. There are all kinds of compost materials around you just going to waste! Check stables for straw and produce companies and grocery stores, restaurants, and the school cafeteria for food wastes. Check to see whether there are any composting guidelines or restrictions in your community before you begin.

Good compost pile materials fall into three categories:

Carbon, or dried matter: dried leaves, straw, dried grass, small branches;

Nitrogen, or fresh matter: kitchen scraps, lawn clippings, leaves, crop leftovers, coffee grounds, weeds (not noxious weeds or those that contain seeds);

Soil/finished compost: both can help to introduce beneficial microorganisms.

Be sure to include plenty of materials from all three categories.

Building Your Compost Pile

Carbon + Nitrogen + Soil/Finished Compost + Air + Water = Compost

Compost is made by layering carbon and nitrogen material in alternating 4- to 6-inch layers. In between these layers you can sprinkle a thin layer of soil or compost. It is also essential to water each layer lightly as you build the pile.

Pile size. The pile should be a minimum of 4 square feet. This size is essential for optimal decomposition and adequate heat retention. Keep the pile under 5 feet high; any higher, and it can become too compressed and deprived of air. However, you can make the pile as long as you want. A properly built pile can heat up to 160°F and destroy many pathogens and weed seeds.

Pile shape. Make the pile rectangular. You can assure this by constantly forking materials out to the corners and edges with each added layer. Without care, the pile can become a giant mound or pyramid rather than the desired 4-foot rectangle, and it will tend to dry up easily.

Aeration. Composting is most efficient when aerobic decomposition (decomposition in the presence of air) is taking place. If the pile is too dense or wet, anaerobic decomposition occurs and produces a strong smell. If anaerobic decomposition develops, turn the pile and add coarse or bulky material, such as straw or twigs.

Moisture. Moisture goes hand in hand with aeration. The pile should be as moist as a wrung-out sponge. A soggy pile encourages anaerobic decomposition. If rain is a problem, put a roof over the compost area or cover the pile with a large tarp.

Size of materials. By chopping up materials, you expose more surface area for the decomposers to work on. The smaller the materials, the faster your pile will decompose. You can chop up the materials with a spade before adding them to the pile.

Involving Students

Building a compost pile is a big job best accomplished by older students or adults. That said, young children can play a role by participating in the following tasks:

* Collecting appropriate food scraps after a class snack (this is easiest if everyone had a snack that was compostable, such as after the class eats apples or bananas).
* Working together to spread straw or dry leaves over food scraps in an established pile.
* Moving weeds from a pile in the garden to the compost pile (have an adult check first that none of the weeds are noxious and all are suitable for the compost).

Ready-to-Use Compost

In general, the pile has finished decomposing when the compost:
– is dark brown and looks like soil
– is composed of nonrecognizable ingredients
– has an earthy, humus-like odor

The exterior of the pile will not fully decompose. Check at least 6 inches into the interior of the pile to observe its characteristics. The entire process will take 3 to 12 months, depending on the type of pile, how you maintain it, and the materials you use.

Once the pile is decomposed, sift it through a heavy-gauge wire screen. It is then ready for use in soil mixes, garden beds, or as a fertilizer around trees, shrubs, and perennial borders. Be generous. An adage recommends that the less your soil looks like compost, the more compost you need to add!

Let Worms Make Your Compost

(Adapted from "Let Worms Make Your Compost," by Martha Brown, University of California, Santa Cruz. Read more organic garden tips at: http://escholarship.org/uc/search?entity=casfs_fg)

Vermicomposting is a simple, efficient composting system that appeals to many people, especially those who mainly have food wastes to compost or a small space in which to compost. Getting started requires only a lidded container, redworms, some bedding for the worms to live in, and food scraps. Maintenance is simple: bury food scraps in the bedding, add new bedding occasionally, and harvest the digested results, known as castings. You can harvest finished worm castings in four months, and these crumbly, brown castings have a higher nutrient content than many other composts.

ALICIA DICKERSON/LIFE LAB

The Worms

Redworms are best suited to vermicomposting for many reasons. Also known as manure worms and red wigglers, redworms thrive in areas with high organic matter. They will naturally colonize a manure or compost pile, as well as areas under trees with high leaf fall, surface feeding in the top 18 inches of material. Redworms, *Eisenia fetida*, are not the same as earthworms and night crawlers, which prefer to construct semipermanent burrows in undisturbed soils.

There are several options for getting a starter batch of redworms: dig them out of a friend's bin (best option); mail-order them; or dig them out of a horse manure pile (when the pile has cooled down). You'll need 1 to 2 pounds of redworms (or about 1,000-2,000 worms) to start an average-size home vermicomposting system. Redworms reproduce rapidly under the right conditions: 8 worms can multiply to 1,500 in six months! In a well-maintained system, redworms can live up to five years.

The Box

You can use many different types of containers for vermicomposting, from wooden boxes to plastic tubs, but to work properly they need the following features:

1. A tight-fitting lid and a bottom for protection from pests and weather;
2. Holes for drainage and aeration;
3. A depth of 12 to 18 inches;
4. Appropriate space for the amount of food waste to be composted.

Redworms do their best work in a dark, damp (but not soggy) environment with temperatures averaging between 55° and 77°F. Lids protect worms from sunlight and its drying heat (and keep rodents and flies away). Bottoms keep out worm-eating moles and other burrowing rodents. In addition, you can move a box indoors onto bricks set above a tray in winter to protect against frost, and into the shade in summer. Drainage holes and aeration holes help keep the box from becoming too soggy (worms can drown!). Containers that are 12 to 18 inches deep work best, since redworms are oxygen-needing surface feeders that won't venture much deeper than 18 inches.

When choosing the size of the box, consider the amount of food scraps generated by your household each week. Mary Appelhof, author of the vermicomposter's bible *Worms Eat My Garbage*, suggests that prospective vermicomposters collect and weigh their food scraps over several weeks before deciding on a box size. She offers this rule of thumb for calculating size: allow 1 square foot of surface area for each pound of food wastes to be added per week. For example, a 2'x4' box has 8 square feet of surface area and can handle 8 pounds of food waste a week (the amount typically produced by two to three adults a week).

Wooden boxes are better suited to vermicomposting than those made of plastic or metal. Wood absorbs and drains excess moisture, while metal and plastic trap moisture inside. Especially in wet climates, plastic worm bins can foster anaerobic conditions due to excess moisture build up and resulting compaction. If using a metal or plastic bin, be sure to drill adequate drainage holes in the bottom and aeration holes in the sides. Beginning vermicomposters can get started in almost any container — plastic laundry tubs, galvanized tin buckets, old bureau drawers, packing crates — before building a more permanent box. You can design wooden boxes, whether made from scrap wood or new plywood and 2x4s, to accommodate your household's specific needs (see Making a Worm Box, p. 117). You can also purchase commercially made bins online or from your waste-management provider.

The Bedding

After you've built or acquired your box, fill it with a 1-foot-deep layer of bedding. Bedding materials such as leaves and shredded newspaper provide worms with a damp, aerated place to live, as well as a food source. Bulky and high in carbon, the bedding materials provide a matrix in which to bury the wet, high-nitrogen food scraps. Composting food scraps without bedding can result in a slimy, smelly mess. Together, the bedding and the food scraps are a balanced compost medium and a balanced diet for the worms. In a few months the worms will eat their way through both the food scraps and the bedding.

Redworms particularly like maple leaves with a bit of soil mixed in. Leaves from other deciduous trees also make great bedding, with the exception of walnut leaves, which contain tannins that are harmful to worms. Other good bedding materials include shredded newspaper or corrugated cardboard torn into 1- to 2-inch-wide strips. Straw works best if mixed with other bedding materials due to its tendency to mat.

All bedding materials must be moist, but not soggy. Worms are 75 to 90 percent moisture, and their skins must be moist to respire (they breathe through their skins). Bedding should be as moist as a wrung-out sponge, or about 70 percent moisture. It's best to soak dry bedding materials (leaves, straw, newspaper), then allow them to drain overnight before adding them to the worm box. If the materials seem too wet, squeeze out excess moisture.

Feeding and Maintaining the Worms

Everyday a redworm eats half its weight in food. They will eat their way through any food waste except hard bones. Fruit and vegetable scraps, grains and breads, coffee grounds, and tea bags are all wonderful worm foods. Worms will also eat meat, dairy products, and oily foods, but if pests and odors are a problem,

avoid putting these scraps in the worm box. Worms have favorite foods and foods they avoid. They will flock to the underside of a melon rind, and may avoid a citrus peel or onion for weeks until bacteria have broken down its caustic substances.

To feed your worms, bury food scraps in holes dug into the bedding. Use a hand fork to open a hole or a small trench in the bedding, dump in the food scraps, and then cover them with a few inches of bedding. Covering the food with bedding and worm castings will help keep flies and odors away. Rotate food burial sites to distribute the food scraps evenly throughout the box.

While worm composting is relatively trouble free, you can avoid a couple of problems by taking simple preventive measures. If a worm box develops smelly, slimy spots, chances are the bin is too wet or has too much food waste in it. Remedy this problem by adding fresh bedding and reducing the amount of wet food you put in the box. Make sure you have adequate drainage and aeration holes. You can avoid fruit flies in summer by covering food wastes with a few inches of bedding and castings. As a second line of defense, cover the bedding with a sheet of plastic, burlap, or canvas and tuck it in around the edges.

Harvesting and Using the Castings

After about four months, the worms will have chewed their way through most of the food scraps and bedding material, leaving behind a boxful of nutrient-rich castings. The easiest way to harvest the castings is by "Dividing and Migrating:" push all the material to one side of the box (side A), then add moist, fresh bedding to the remaining space (side B). Bury food only in the new bedding in side B. Over the next six weeks to two months, the worms will migrate from the old material and castings in side A to the new food and bedding in side B. Once you've removed the castings from side A, you can add fresh bedding and start burying food on side A only. This method will give you a new supply of worm castings about every four months and will keep your worms healthy and productive.

The harvested castings look dark and crumbly and should smell like good soil. High in nitrogen and phosphorus and a great source of organic matter, castings are wonderful additions to potting mixes for seeds, transplants, or houseplants. You can also use castings like compost in vegetable and flower beds, as a cover soil for seed beds, and as a top dressing for perennials.

Worm Compost Related Activities

❀ A Home for the Worms, p. 41
❀ Harvesting Worm Castings, p. 43

Tips for Creating a Healthy Garden Ecosystem

(Adapted with permission from the California School Garden Network's book,
Gardens for Learning: Creating and Sustaining School Gardens)

Healthy gardens start with healthy soil, which makes for healthy plants. Just like healthy people ward off illness, healthy plants are less susceptible to pests and disease. Giving back to the soil in the form of compost is one way to maintain healthy soil and feed beneficial soil microorganisms. Fertilizers are another way to help plants stay healthy, but fertilizers cannot "build" and improve soil as compost does.

ALICIA DICKERSON/LIFE LAB

Monitor for Pests

Garden ecosystems provide homes for all types of bugs, good ones (pollinators and predators of pests) and bad ones (pests) alike. Maintaining a balance of these critters in your garden's ecosystem is important.

Observe plants for plant-eating insects like aphids and scales (they often hide under the leaves). If found early, you can control their populations through hand-picking or by using a high-pressure water spray.

Remove any leaves with signs of disease so it does not spread as irrigation and rainwater bounce off the plants. If you remove diseased plants, it is best not to place them in your compost pile.

When you find signs of pests, your first step should be to identify what is causing the problem. This can be an exciting investigative activity for students. Once your sleuths identify the problem, decide whether the damage is significant enough to warrant action.

Tolerate some plant damage. Observing the interactions in a garden ecosystem is an important part of the learning process for your students. Many plant pests have natural predators, and if you remove the pests, your students will never get to see the predators in action. For example, ladybugs are ferocious aphid consumers. However, with no aphid population, you won't attract any ladybugs.

If the damage becomes more severe, decide whether or not the plants are worth keeping. Disease problems are often a sign that the plants are not well adapted to their environment, so replacing them with crops better suited to the location may be the easiest solution. In addition to monitoring the plants and providing proper maintenance to promote good plant health, here are some other techniques to minimize pest and disease buildup in the garden.

Promote a Healthy Garden Environment

Practice crop rotation. Pests and diseases that affect certain crops (or families of crops) build up in the soil if the same crop is grown in a particular bed year after year. By rotating crops on a three-year cycle — planting a different crop in the bed each year — you can avoid many problems.

Discourage excess moisture on foliage. Most fungal and bacterial diseases can infect plant surfaces only if there is moisture present. In regions where the growing season is humid, provide adequate space between plants so that air can circulate freely. Try to keep students out of the garden when it's wet so they don't inadvertently spread disease organisms. It's best to water in the morning, and don't water tomatoes, potatoes, squash, and cucumbers from above.

Plant disease- and pest-resistant varieties. Some varieties of crops are naturally less susceptible to problems, and plant breeders have developed many others. Look for resistance information in catalog variety descriptions and on seed packets.

Plant appropriate varieties for your area and growing season. Many plants will not thrive if they are grown in the wrong climate, zone, or time of year.

Clean up your garden. Diseases and pests can remain on infected and dead plant material, making it easy for them to attack other plants. Remove infected plant leaves, keep weeds to a minimum, and clean up the garden at the end of the growing season.

Encourage beneficial organisms. Make the garden inviting to pest predators (good bugs) such as ladybugs, wasps, lacewings, and birds. To attract insect predators and parasites, plant "insectary" plants and flowers that provide moisture, shelter for alternative prey, and immediate nutrition from nectar (carbohydrates) and pollen (protein).

Many insectary plants are common garden varieties of cut flowers, herbs, vegetables, and ornamentals. Establishing perennial plantings in your garden is one way to create a healthy garden ecosystem. Consult with your local nursery professional or master gardener for suggestions of good insectary plants.

Practice Pest Control
USE BARRIERS
* *Gopher wire:* Use galvanized mesh wire with openings no larger than 3/4 inch. For in-ground beds, dig out the bed to a depth of at least one foot. Lay wire on the bottom of the bed and up all the sides, making sure the edges come up to ground level. If you need to overlap pieces of wire, overlap them by 1 foot. The deeper you bury the wire, the less chance there will be of catching or tearing it with digging tools. In a raised bed container, staple wire to the bottom of the bed frame. Install gopher baskets around the root balls of trees and perennial plantings.
* *Row covers:* Place floating row covers made of lightweight fabric over plants to protect them from invading pests. The fabric allows light, moisture, and air to pass through. However, if you cover a crop that requires insect pollination in order to bear fruit, you will have to remove the covers when the plants begin to blossom. Row

covers may also deter some animal pests, but fences are often the only way to keep large, persistent creatures out of the garden. Use netting to protect fruit crops from hungry birds.
* *Collars:* Prevent cutworm damage by making a collar of newspaper, stiff paper, or boxboard that circles seedling stalks and extends 2 inches above and below ground.

USE HOMEMADE INSECTICIDES
* *Soap water solution:* Mix 1 tablespoon of dishwashing soap (Ivory works best) in 1 quart of water. Put in a spray bottle and spray all plant surfaces, including the undersides of leaves. Good for aphids and white flies. Rinse food before eating.
* *Hot pepper solution:* Use a blender to prepare a mixture of 1 hot pepper, 2 cloves of garlic, and 4 cups of water. Strain, put in a spray bottle, and spray all plant surfaces, including the undersides of leaves. Good for insect pests. Rinse food before eating.

USE TRAPS
* *Hose or newspaper:* A short section of old hose or a rolled up newspaper attracts nighttime pests like earwigs. In the morning, collect and move them out of the garden.
* *Boards:* Use a board laid on the soil with a little bit of crawl space beneath to collect snails and slugs. In the morning you can gather and carry them far from the vegetable garden, squash them, or feed them to some chickens. Hand picking snails and slugs in the evening or early morning works well, too.
* *Animal traps:* Trap gophers and moles or other animal pests with care. The cinch trap is one of the best traps sold. Use caution since these traps can injure hands if handled improperly. Only adults should use these types of traps and be sure to check on school policies regarding the use of rodent traps.

REMOVE PESTS
* *Handpicking:* Often the easiest and best defense is to hand pick insect pests off plants. Squeamish gardeners may prefer to use gloves. Dispose of pests by squashing them, drowning them in a container of soapy water, or carrying them to another area.
* *High-pressure sprays:* Spraying infested plants with water at a high pressure can effectively wash off insect populations such as aphids, drowning them in the process. You may have to repeat this process

Building a Coldframe for Your Garden

A coldframe is a protective structure, like a greenhouse on a very small scale, that can extend your growing season into the colder months of winter and give you a head start on seedlings before spring has officially arrived.

You can build many different types of coldframes, depending on your needs and budget. Following is a design for a simple one. Try to recycle materials if possible. You can use excess lumber and plastic film, or build your coldframe using old windows. Situate coldframes so that they face south to receive at least 6 hours of direct sunlight during the spring and fall. Most of all, coldframes should be accessible, in areas where students can reach, water, observe, and work within them with ease.

You can grow almost anything inside a coldframe, although it is best to stay away from plants that spread out when growing, such as peas or melons. Instead, try leafy greens for fresh salads in the wintertime, and start seedlings for early spring crops. Grow tomatoes and peppers in late summer for a fall crop.

Some Points to Remember

Since gardening in coldframes is intensive and requires nutrient-rich soil, it's a good idea to add some compost to the soil to enrich it.

Temperatures in a coldframe can get quite hot if it is not ventilated properly. Place a thermometer inside to help you regulate temperatures. Ventilate when necessary by opening vents or lifting sides of plastic, opening windows, and so on. The best coldframe temperatures for growing most plants can differ from regular outdoor gardening. Cool-season plants grow well with coldframe temperatures of 45° to 70°F (7.2° to 21.1°C); warm-weather plants at 75° to 85°F (23.4° to 29.4°C).

To increase heat retention during very cold weather, place coldframes 8 to 10 inches (20 to 25 cm) in the ground or paint the insides black. Plastic jugs filled with water placed inside the coldframe also help to increase heat retention. On very cold nights, you can cover the coldframe with straw or even blankets. Since coldframes help retain water, be very careful not to overwater. Overwatering can cause mildew and mold to grow and ruin your crops. Water condensation inside the coldframe is a sign of overwatering. If you raise the north side of the coldframe 6 inches (15.2 cm) above the south side, it will shed rainwater and retain heat better.

A Simple Coldframe Design

This design yields a 4'x7' coldframe, about 2 feet high at the back edge.

MATERIALS

* Lumber (preferably redwood or other weather-resistant wood; do not use pressure-treated wood)
* 4 3" x 1 1/2" hinges
* 4 L-brackets
* 7 4" flat brackets
* 2 7'-long 2x12s
* 2 4'-long 2x12s
* 1 7'-long 2x10
* 2 tapered 4'-long 2x10s
* 4 3 1/2'-long 1x2s
* 4 44"-long 1x2s
* Tacks
* 2 1/2" nails
* 1" screws
* 2 3 1/2'x4' pieces polyethylene film or plastic
* Hammer
* Screwdriver
* Foam insulation strips (weatherstripping)
* Thermometer

STEP 1:

Frame the base of the coldframe using 2x12 boards as per the diagram. Add L-brackets to each inside corner for stability.

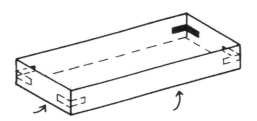

STEP 2:

Use the flat brackets and 1" screws to add the tapered boards and back piece (2x10s) to the base to add height to the coldframe.

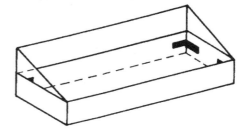

STEP 3:

Frame the covers as per the diagram. Then tack plastic film to the outside of each cover.

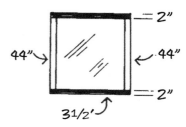

STEP 4:

Using hinges, attach the cover to the top of the back side of the coldframe.

Note: Add foam insulation strips on frame below cover if necessary to add insulation and cut down on heat loss.

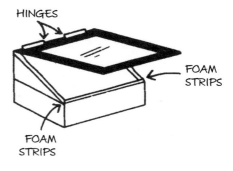

STEP 5:

Add thermometer to inside back wall so that it is easy to read.

Note: Use small sticks to prop open the cold-frame for ventilation. Mound soil around its edges for added insulation.

Root View Boxes

WAYS TO USE ROOT VIEW BOXES

❋ Show the movement of water through various kinds of soils.

❋ Show how water moves through soil layers.

❋ Show how the roots and the top of a plant change their growth when the box is laid on its side after the plant has developed in the upright position.

❋ Compare and contrast different root types.

MILK-CARTON ROOT VIEW BOXES

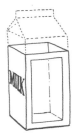

1. Cut the top (for a vertical box) or the side (for a horizontal box) from a half-gallon (1.89L) milk carton.

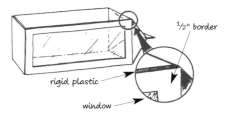

2. Cut out a window area leaving about 1/2 inch (1.3 cm) of carton between the corner and the window. Cut a piece of rigid plastic to fit tightly into the corners of the carton. Use waterproof glue or pruning paint for a tighter seal.

3. Since roots tend to grow straight down, the window must be slanted (the carton tipped) to keep roots growing against the glass, with all of their action visible.

ROOT VIEW CUPS

1. Use clear plastic 8- to 10-oz cups.

2. Cut out a paper sleeve for each root view cup.

The sleeve will be used to block light. To make a template for the sleeves, cut straight down one side of a cup, then cut off the bottom and the top rim. You should end up with an arch shape that you can lay flat and trace onto dark construction paper. Experiment with elongating one end of the arch to create a sleeve that can overlap at the seam and be taped. Tape the sleeve around the cup to block light.

3. Punch three holes in the bottom of each cup for drainage — any sharp tool works, but a drill is quick and easy.

BUILDING A ROOT VIEW BOX

Using the diagram below, you can create an educational structure for your garden. Attach two 5'-long 2x4s to the sides of the finished box to mount it in the garden, or place your box on a table top. It is a good idea to treat the wood with a wood-preserving oil, such as tung oil, before filling it with soil. Fill the box to the top with a mixture of half garden soil and half compost, or use a potting soil mix. Plant seeds right up against the rigid plastic window. Keep the soil moist but not soggy and watch your seeds sprout and the roots grow.

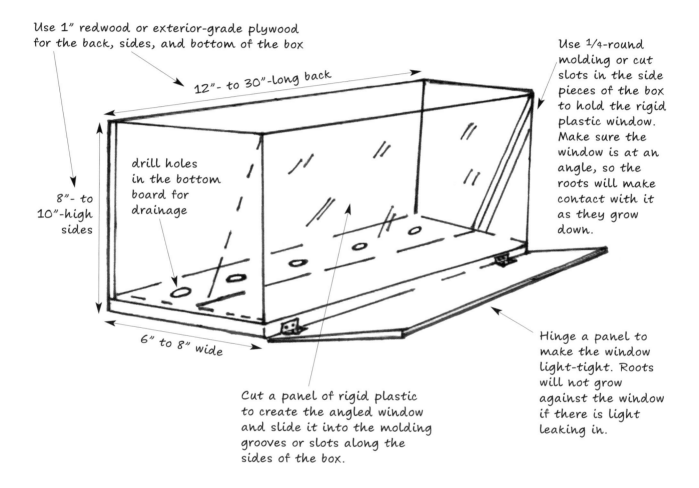

Use 1" redwood or exterior-grade plywood for the back, sides, and bottom of the box

12"- to 30"-long back

8"- to 10"-high sides

drill holes in the bottom board for drainage

6" to 8" wide

Use 1/4-round molding or cut slots in the side pieces of the box to hold the rigid plastic window. Make sure the window is at an angle, so the roots will make contact with it as they grow down.

Hinge a panel to make the window light-tight. Roots will not grow against the window if there is light leaking in.

Cut a panel of rigid plastic to create the angled window and slide it into the molding grooves or slots along the sides of the box.

WHAT TO PLANT

Large seeds such as beans make for good germination viewing. Fava or bell beans develop easy-to-see root nodules that are used to fix nitrogen. Rainbow chard and nigella plants have colored roots, which make for interesting viewing. Plant a variety of seeds and compare the different root structures.

TIPS FOR ANY ROOT VIEW BOX

❀ Roots will not grow in light. Make sure your window is covered when not viewing roots.
❀ Plant seeds right up against the window or the side of the cup.

Plans for a Planter Box
48"l x 11½"h x 20¾"w

These plans are for a box that you could set on top of concrete. For this project, we recommend using weather-resistant wood, such as redwood, cedar, or plastic lumber; do not use pressure-treated wood due to its toxicity.

MATERIALS
* 2 4'-long 1x12s
* 2 20¾"-long 1x12s
* 2 4'-long 1x10s
* 5 19"-long 2x4s
* 1¾" nails or screws
* Hammer or screwdriver
* 5'x 2½' rectangular piece of gopher wire
* Staple gun and staples
* Work gloves

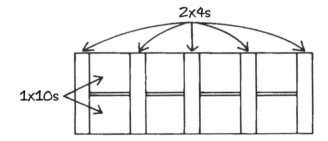

BOTTOM
Place the two 1x10s next to each other, leaving a small space between them. Nail the five pieces of 2x4s to the 1x10 slats, spacing them evenly.

SIDES
Attach the four 1x12 side pieces, nailing them into the bottom 1x10 slats *and* the 2x4s to form a box.

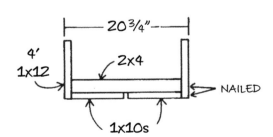

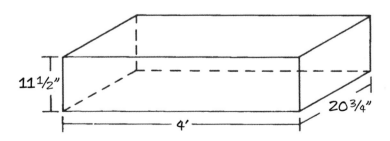

Making a Worm Box

A house for me?

MATERIALS

* One 4' x 8' sheet of plywood
* 2 20"-long 2x4s for lid
* 2 45"-long 2x4s for lid
* 1 20"-long 2x4 for base frame
* 2 23"-long 2x4s for base frame
* 2 39"-long 2x4s for base frame
* 16d nails

STEP 1:

Measure the sheet of plywood using the template at right, and cut out the pieces.

24"	24"	23"	24"
END (16")	END	BASE	LID
SIDE (16")			
SIDE (16")		WASTE	

42"

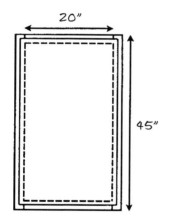

20"

45"

STEP 2:

Make the lid frame out of 2x4s lying flat, using 2 16d nails at each joint. Then attach the plywood lid as shown (left).

STEP 3:

Make the base frame out of 2x4s standing on edge, using 2 16d nails at each joint. Then attach the plywood base and drill 1/4" drainage holes in the base as shown (right). Attach side and end pieces to the base.

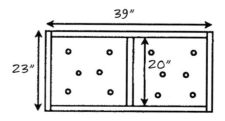

39"

23"   20"

Insect Collecting Net

Students may enjoy catching insects around the garden for a closer look. To use the net, move it slowly underneath a flying insect, then lift quickly, turning the net over as you lift so that the insect doesn't fly out.

MATERIALS (for one net)

* ❋ 1 52" length of #8 iron wire
* ❋ 1 1"diameter, 4"-long piece of aluminum tubing or PVC pipe
* ❋ 1 7/8" diameter, 3'-long wood dowel
* ❋ 1 48"x30" piece of muslin
* ❋ 1 very small screw
* ❋ Pliers
* ❋ Utility knife
* ❋ Duct tape
* ❋ Needle and thread

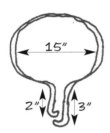

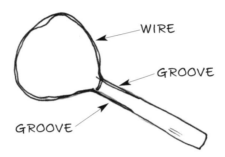

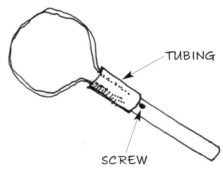

STEP 1: Use pliers to bend the wire as shown.

STEP 2: Carefully cut 2 grooves along dowel (down a few inches from the top) to hold the wire against the wood. Secure the wire firmly by wrapping with duct tape.

STEP 3: Slide the piece of aluminum tubing or PVC over the dowel, wires, and duct tape to secure them. Use the small screw to keep the tubing from slipping.

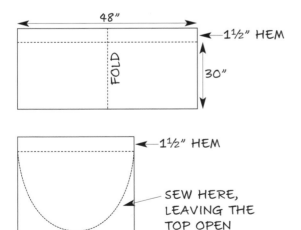

STEP 4: Fold the muslin and sew as shown, leaving a 1¹/₂" hem.

STEP 5: Hem the muslin around the wire and you've got an insect collecting net!

English/Spanish Vocabulary List

Translated by Francisco Javier Espinoza

KEY
(a) = adjective
(n) = noun
(v) = verb
[ ] = words between brackets are not a direct
    translation, but they are frequently used
    in the same sense

A

abdomen abdomen, vientre, [panza]

adaptation adaptación, ajuste

advertisement anuncio

advertising publicado (n), anunciando (v)

agriculture agricultura

air aire

air pressure presión de aire

amino acids aminoácidos

animals animales

antennae antenas

atmosphere atmósfera

B

barometer barómetro

beds camas, camas agricolas

C

calcium calcio

calories calorías

carbohydrate carbohidrato, hidrato de carbono

carbon dioxide dióxido de carbono

carnivore carnívoro

change cambio

chlorophyll clorofila

circle círculo, [rueda]

clay arcilla, barro

climate clima

cloud nube

cold frío

communication comunicación

community comunidad

compaction compactacíon, apisonamiento

companion acompanante, compañero or compañera

compost composta

compromise compromiso

consumer consumidor

"control" (for experiment) testigo

convection convección

cooperation cooperación

consumerism el consumo

crop cultivo

cycle ciclo

D

deciduous decíduo, cáduco

decision decisión

decomposers detritívoros, descomponedores

decomposition descomposición, degradación

degrees grados

depend depender (v)

depth profundidad, hondura

development desarrollo

drain drenaje

E

earthworm lombriz de tierra

ecosystem ecosistema

embryo embrión

encouragement apoyo, estimulación, animar

energy energía

environment medio ambiente

evaporation evaporación

exchange intercambio

exoskeleton exoesqueleto

F

farmer agricultor, campesino, [ranchero]

fat gordo (a), grasa (n)

filament filamento, [hilo]

flat (seedling tray) cajita para sembrar

flower flor

fog niebla, neblina

food comida, alimento

food chain cadena, alimenticia

fuel combustible

fungi hongos

G

garbage basura, desperdicio

garden jardín

gases gases

geotropism geotropismo

germination germinación

grain grano

gravity gravedad

greenhouse invernadero

group grupo

growth crecimiento

H

habitat hábitat

hail saludar (v), vitorear (v), granizo(n)

harvest cosecha (n), cosechar (v)

hear oir (v)

heat calentar (v), calor (n)

herbivore herbívoro

hot caliente

humans humanos

humidity humedad

humus humus, [tierra negra]

hydrotropism hidrotropismo

I

ingredients ingredientes

insect insecto

insulation aislamiento, térmico o eléctrico

interrelationship correlación, relación mutua, interrelación

iron hierro, fierro

J

jaw mandíbula, quijada

L

leaf hoja

M

maintenance mantenimiento

manure guano, boñiga, [caca de ganado o gallinas]

meat-eater carnívoro

microclimate microclima

milk leche

minerals minerales

mold moho

molecules moléculas

mouth boca

N

nitrogen nitrógeno

nutrients nutrientes

nutrition nutrición

O

ovary ovario

oxygen oxígeno ["aire"]

P

pests plagas

petal pétalo

phosphorus fósforo

photosynthesis fotosíntesis

phototropism fototropismo

pistil pistilo

planting siembra, plantar, sembrando

plants plantas

poison veneno, ponzoña

pollen polen

pollination polinización

potassium potasio

predator predador

prey presa

process proceso

producers productores

protein proteína

psychrometer psicrómetro

R

radiation radiación

rain lluvia

rain gauge pluviómetro

rake rastrillo

recycle reciclar, reusar

reflection reflexión

resources recursos

root raíz

S

safety seguridad

salt sal

sand arena

seasons estaciones del año

seed coat cubierta de semilla, cáscara de semilla

seedling plántula, [plantita]

seeds semillas

senses sentidos

sepal sépalo

shade sombra

shovel pala

sight sentido de Ia vista, vistazo, visión

silt limo

sleet granizo

smell olfato (n), oler (v)

soil suelo, tierra

solar solar

solar collector colector solar

spacing espaciar, espaciamiento

spading fork trinche, rastrillo

stamen estambre

starch almidón

style estilo

sugar azúcar

support apoyo (n), apoyar (v)

systems sistemas injerto (n)

T

taste sentido de gusto, saborear (v) [probar (v)]

temperature temperatura

texture textura

thermometer termómetro

thigmotropism tigmotropismo

thorax tórax, torso

tool herramienta

topsoil capa superior del suelo

touch tacto (n), tocar (v), toque (n)

transpiration transpiración, sudar

transplant transplantar (v), transplante (n)

trophic levels niveles tróficos

V

variety variedad

vegetable verdura

vegetarian vegetariano or vegetarian

Vitamin A vitamina A

Vitamin C vitamina C

vitamins vitaminas

W

warm tibio(a), cálido(a)

weather tiempo ["clima"]

weeds malezas, hierbas

wheelbarrow carretilla

wind viento ["aire"]

wind meter anemómetro

wind vane veleta

wing ala